To Know Is To Know That You Don't Know

by

Sebastian James Rozo

"Lies will flow from my lips, but there may perhaps be some truth mixed up with them; it is for you to seek out this truth and to decide whether any part of it is worth keeping. If not, you will of course throw the whole of it into the wastepaper basket and forget all about it."

+ Virginia Woolf

"Be it life or death, we crave only reality."

+ Henry David Thoreau

Prologue

To All,

As I delicately write this, on what could be considered my death-desk—the desk that I will soon die on—I am simultaneously fulfilling my last desire on this wonderful planet, which is:

To create a book of selected entries from my greatest student's journals.

You see, in a month spent studying with me, each student was required to write down their every day experiences, feelings, and insights. In this way, they were able to be more aware of their internal movements and the made-up identity that those movements seem to create. So, for all practical purposes, we will call this made-up identity we all seem to believe in: **the believed-to-be-self.**

This believed-to-be-self is the fictional identity we as human beings perceive our true nature to be, thus explaining most of our confusions, depressions, irritations, feelings of lack, feelings of purposelessness, and the general, unexplained frustration many of us feel on a day-to-day basis.

We all know deep down that there is more to Life than this believed-to-be-self allows us to see.

And thus, this book is the result of such explorations.

With Freedom & Love Beyond Belief,

Wy

CHAPTER
396 Hz

Miro's Notebook

January 3rd, 30__

+ The longer I live, the more I feel like I'm living within a soap bubble dream.

Whose soap bubble dream is it persay?

I do not know.

Yet, there seems to be extensive similarities between this seemingly solid, physical Waking State we call: *Real Life*

And that of the ephemeral, fluid, and fantastical Dream State we call: *Dreaming.*

The thing is this:

I keep dreaming situations in the Dream State that feel *as if* they were actually happening to me in Real Life.

And not only situations, but I also find myself thinking and believing similar thoughts in the Dream State as I would think and believe in Real Life.

I then wake up and realize all of it was only a dream—a transitory state of forms loosely mimicking my Real Life environment and its creative narratives.

I wake up and feel like the entire dreaming experience was like a huge soap bubble that was just popped.

Poof! Pop! Gone.

All of this naturally leads me to question my "Real Life" and my corresponding perceptions of it.

Is this all just a dream as well?

Is our Real Life comparable to an enormous soap bubble, composed out of many smaller soap bubbles, that includes:

Our thoughts, our words, our actions, our friends, our family, strangers, situations, locations, and even ourselves waiting to be popped at some point?

Is our Real Life just a more solid-looking-and-feeling dream that we ascribe all this permanency and seriousness to while distracting ourselves from the transient and playful essence of Life?

Isn't this all going to end at some point anyways?

What happens then?

* * *

Thoroughly reflecting on these questions, how does one now live out their "Real Life?"

Wouldn't one attempt to get to the bottom of these questions and investigate the origin of our transitory beliefs?

Our thoughts…?

DREAMING THE DREAM

January 6th, 30__

+ Everything seems to resemble a dream,

Everything with dream-like qualities,

Memories and their ephemerality, conversations, thoughts, emotions.

Transitory, fleeting, momentary.

Even these words, they're essentially written down to prolong the seeming permanence of this message.

If these words weren't written down in a coherent form and/or syntax then the thought would've just passed by and travelled back to its Source.

So, in a more distilled sense, almost everything we say and do originates from our thoughts that are just as momentary as what we say and do.

So, you ask, what's the point of writing all of this down then?

Well, it feels right.

It satisfies something in this unique moment.

It feels as if these thoughts should be shared with Others.

And that's what I feel Art consists of:

Sharing our greatest thoughts, and their eventual shaping into physical manifestations, with Others.

What else would you do if you felt your Life to be but a dream?

* * *

Now, imagine what a dream feels like when you're in it.

Now, imagine what it feels like when you're out of it.

Now, imagine the same feeling of being in a dream but in your current Real Life.

What would you do?

Is there even a permanent "you?"

If the person you thought you were in a dream just poofs when you wake up, couldn't the same thing happen to you now in your "Real Life" too?

"The thing that I have the greatest difficulty in believing in, is my own reality. I am constantly getting outside myself, and as I watch myself act I cannot understand how a person who acts is the same as the person who is watching him act, and who wonders in astonishment and doubt how he can be actor and watcher at the same moment."

+ Andre Gide

REMEMBERISM

January 8th, 30__

"There is either life or death.
And while we are alive, we might as well learn what that means."

+ Matthew McCarthy

+ I'm naively creating a new label for an ancient practice,

It's going to be called: *Rememberism*.

Reminiscent of: *Memento Mori*: a medieval Christian practice of reflecting on one's death, Rememberism echoes Seneca's, Marcus Aurelius', & Socrates' perspectives on the shortness and fortune of being alive.

What is Rememberism's premise?

To continuously, and responsibly, remind one's self of one's inevitable death, using this unwavering reflection as a way to improve one's current perceptions and overall quality of Life.

Side effects can include:

- Cutting through any delusional beliefs that don't serve you anymore.

- Increasing your appreciation for the sheer fortune of being alive.

- Spurring any unused creativity into action.

- Catalyzing anything that you've wanted to begin for a while now, but have suppressed due to limitations you've put upon yourself.

Or any combo of these,

Death: the Greatest Mystery of Life, is a Teacher patiently waiting to be reflected upon to further reveal Life's Fullest Grandeur to us.

> "We do not know where death awaits us:
> so let us wait for it everywhere.
> To practise death is to practise freedom."
>
> + Michel de Montaigne

LIFE'S RECURRING ORGASM

January 9th, 30__

+ All speech is, is performance.

And we are all just Performers performing in this awe-inspiring Amalgam of Awe.

One never truly knows where one's locus is located in this Beautiful Fluxing of the Flux.

A state of constant departure intermingled with the feeling of having just arrived is the Recurring Feeling.

And one never knows where it begins, nor ends.

It is always Just Right Here, continuously,

As if reliving the couple seconds of space—during and after one has orgasmed—over, and over, and over again.

> "One Moment in Annihilation's Waste,
> One Moment, of the Well of Life to taste—"
>
> + Omar Khayyam, *Rubaiyat*

January 12th, 30__

+ Does jazz music gets jazzed about itself?

    If a table could talk, would it talk?

    If a man is alive, could he also be dead?

    If a man were dead, could he also be alive?

    Does this piece of paper care what's written on it?

    Does this plastic pen care about what it writes?

    Does the essence of the paper change when written on?

    Does the same ever change the same?

    Does change ever change differently?

January 15th, 30__

* * *

Pen penning.

Paper papering.

The Process continues.

***

+ Words want to come out one way, yet they come out another.

As information from the world makes its way into our internal world,

We take a fraction of that information and attempt to assimilate it with the information we already have within us.

From this process, perceptions and interpretations are born.

We interpret our perceptions in one way, only to change them at a later date.

So why do we take our perceptions of the world so seriously when they come and go as guests in the summertime,

When they come and go as the microscopic flickerings of a flame,

When they come and go as the glistening morning dew on fragile blades of grass.

People have duped themselves for so long that they take their perceptions of the world—and their believed-to-be-self—to be the foundation of their Reality.

They continuously construct unique narratives, made out of their thoughts, ideas, conditionings, and experiences as the basis of how they move in the world and how they live within themselves.

So, with this, we must all tread lightly when questioning Other's perspectives.

And we must be careful when negotiating Reality with Others.

Some are not ready.

And you yourself might not be either.

The Fire comes for everyone in Its Own Timing…

THE FIRE

January 17th, 30__

+ The Fire comes for everyone.

It roars and crepitates in celebration of the burning,
the transmutation to be.

Thoughts want to keep the believed-to-be-self narrative going,
while The Fire cannot wait to transform it all into colorless ash,

Relaying its urgent message through gaps in the crackles:

Let go.

Freedom!

I see it!

~~~~~~~~~~~~

Gone.

MAZING

January 18th, 30__

+ What are the point of these letters, these words, these sentences, these paragraphs?

Will they get "me" to "my" destination?

Is the destination really "mine" or does it belong to a series of thoughts seducing their way to an imagined destination?

Do I know things because I *actually* know them or do I know things because I pretend to know them?

We live each day repeating our own self-imposed limitations that we hardly recognize anymore because they have become such a habit to believe in that we naturally accept these self-imposed limitations as part of our Reality.

Which thoughts and beliefs do I frequently repeat that limit me in some way?

What areas of my Life do I limit myself the most?

Where do I visibly lack in effortlessness?

What can I subtract in my Life to add more clarity?

* * *

Again, why am I writing all of this?

What is the importance?

Is it for the possible fame one day?

That the "Venerable Miro" once wrote these timeless words for Others to read, resonate with, and somehow alter their misconceptions of Reality?

Is it to help guide myself out of my own maze?

Is it to help guide Others out of their maze?

Why write?

Why?!

"Finding myself quite empty, with nothing to write about, I offered my self to myself as theme and subject matter."

+ Michel de Montaigne

A DIALOGUE WITH MASTER WY

January 21st, 30__

Miro: Master, how does one escape this maze?

Master Wy: What maze Miro?

Miro: The Matrix, Master. Our world.

Master Wy: And where might this "Matrix" be located Miro?

Miro: Here, all around us.

Master Wy: (*looks around*) Where?

Miro: Here!

This tree, that flower, this pen, this very shirt.

All a part of The Matrix.

Master Wy: I see.

And how are we able to experience this "Matrix?"

Miro: (*thinking*) I guess our bodies.

Our senses.

Master Wy: Okay.

So, who's the one experiencing all of this then?

Miro: Me, Miro.

Master Wy: And how do you know you're in fact *Miro*?

Miro: Well, Master, I'm talking to you, no?

I'm hearing you, I'm seeing you, I'm now touching you, I'm sensing you.

The only thing is that I'm not tasting you, but I think that can be excused.

Master Wy: (*laughs*) So you're Miro because of your senses?

Miro: Yeah, I guess.

Master Wy: Well, what if you go blind, are you still Miro?

Miro: Yup, I've still got my other senses.

Master Wy: Well, what if you go deaf as well, are you still Miro?

Miro: Yeah.

Master Wy: Well, what if you can't smell anymore as well, are you still Miro?

Miro: Yeah.

Master Wy: Well, what if you can't touch, taste, or even sense anything anymore as well?

Are you still Miro?

Miro: Well…

No, I guess not…

And that means I wouldn't be able to feel my body anymore, so I can't really say my body is Miro either.

Oh! But, I still have my thoughts though!

Master Wy: True, you do.

So, knowing now that you can't rely on your senses or body to properly explain who Miro is, would you say that you are truly Miro because of your thoughts?

Miro = your thoughts?

Miro: Yeah, that sounds about right.

Master Wy: Have you ever changed your mind before?

Miro: Yes, I have.

Master Wy: Why?

Miro: (*thinking*) Because I had new information that replaced out-of-date information.

Master Wy: And how was this process done?

Miro: Through thinking.

Master Wy: So, how do you expect Miro to be an actual person if he can just be substituted with new and better information—thoughts—at any second?

Miro: But…I'm Miro.

How can I ever forget myself?

Master Wy: To be clear:

You said that you, Miro, are your thoughts,

And you said that you, Miro, are capable of changing your mind—which is, changing your thoughts.

This implies that Miro is as fleeting and temporary as the thoughts that appear in one's mind.

Which then naturally begs the question:

Does Miro actually exist?

Or is he just *another thought* as well?

(silence)

We established that Miro cannot be the body.

We established that Miro cannot be the senses.

Now, we are establishing that Miro cannot be thoughts either.

Then, my good friend, I sincerely ask you:

Who is Miro?

Miro: *(speechless)*

(silence)

Master Wy: This story might help:

"Zen master Baoche of Mount Mayu was fanning himself. A monk approached and said, 'Master, the nature of wind is permanent and there is no place it does not reach. Why, then, do you fan yourself?'

'Although you understand that the nature of the wind is permanent,' Baoche replied, 'you do not understand the meaning of its reaching everywhere.'

'What is the meaning of its reaching everywhere?' asked the monk again.

The master just kept fanning himself.

The monk bowed deeply."

Miro: Master, what do you mean?

Master Wy: Lead your own self out the maze Miro.

Miro: Yes, but how?

Master Wy: By coming to your own conclusions.

Miro: My conclusion is that my conclusions keep changing!

Master Wy: (*laughing*) Good.

Stay with that conclusion for now.

All else will proceed from there.

Miro: I feel like everything is like that anyways, always changing.

Master Wy: You are both correct and not correct.

The believed-to-be-self—the person you think you are, the ego—is in reality nothing more than an accumulation of things (appearances, sensations, memories, experiences, perceptions, and thoughts) that one clings onto and crafts a seemingly continuous identity out of.

This inevitably happens over the course of our lives where more and more layers of complexity accumulate into a personality.

Miro: Hmm, so that explains the everything always changing part, but then how does that explain the me not being correct part?

Master Wy: There is also *something* that is never changing.

Miro: What is it?

(*silence*)

Master Wy: It is a different identity,

One that is more immediate and sincere than the believed-to-be-self appears to be,

An identity which can best be described as:

Awareness.

Miro: And how do you define: *Awareness*, Master?

(*silence*)

Master Wy: It goes beyond words, definitions, concepts, and such.

I can somewhat point to it, but I can never give it to you Miro.

Miro: How come?

Master Wy: You are already it.

Miro: I don't feel like *it*.

Mastery Wy: Too much Miro-ness is in the way. Get out of the way.

Think of Awareness as this:

The awareness of your awareness.

That's it.

Miro: Okay…

Master Wy: Everything else comes after this Awareness.

Our thoughts, our perceptions, our sensations, are all secondary.

With this awareness of our Awareness, it is then easier to distinguish the difference in our identity between:

The identity created by identifying with the thoughts running through our mind,

And the identity of Awareness, which is aware of—and not identifying itself as—these thoughts running through our mind.

It is a subtle difference Miro.

Less cryptically said, once you are able to shift your identity from:

The one created from identifying as your thoughts, (the believed-to-be-self),

To our ever-present identity: the awareness of our ability to be aware—the same identity and capability we as humans all share—(Awareness),

The clearer one understands the games and confusion we've been creating for ourselves.

This Masterpiece of Life naturally becomes lighter, brighter, and easier to enjoy.

Miro: So, okay, hold on, essentially what you're saying is that we are not our thoughts?

Master Wy: Yes.

Miro: And that our minds are ultimately limited?

Master Wy: Yes, the highest conclusion one's mind can conclude is concluding that it is ultimately limited.

Miro: (*a pause*) I'm still confused Master.

A POEM BEFORE MY DAILY MINI-DEATH (SLEEP)

January 24th, 30__
12:22 A.M.

+ Why do I consistently lie to myself?

Begin using the scenes and situations Life offers me to tell the truth more consistently.

Use these same opportunities to allow Others to express their honestly as well.

Honesty cuts through all formalities and masks we use to lubricate our social interactions.

People are craving for any slice of Honesty, Sincerity, and/or Love they can get closest to right now.

You are the catalyst—the push Others need—to go to the next level of Honesty, Sincerity, and/or Love they never believed socially and/or personally possible.

And it all begins with ending the lies we tell ourselves and those we tell Others.

January 25th, 30__

"From books all I seek is to give myself pleasure from an honorable pastime: or if I do study, I seek only that branch of learning which deals with knowing myself and which teaches me how to live and die well."

+ Michel de Montaigne

+ One reads books in order to find the perfectly ordered words that will liberate one out of their current imprisonment of understanding.

Meaning: we read so we can find the perfect sentence(s) that will show us a freer way to think about something.

When we habitually think about a subject over and over again, it's easy to think about it in the same exact way, with the same associated thoughts.

This dynamic reveals the importance of thinking freely and the healing capabilities of spontaneity—in whichever form they take.

In regards to books and the liberating thoughts they offer, one must continuously remember that these messages are temporary keys that unlock various levels of Understanding, leading to higher and more profound Understandings beyond the previous ones known.

In its bare essence, each liberating Understanding has both the capability to entrap one in that level or take one to the next level.

It is up to you and you alone.

Another way of framing this phenomenon is by either viewing each liberating thought as:

A new ship that slowly begins deteriorating,

Or a new ship that keeps transforming itself with more efficient sails, sturdier wood. and a better steering system.

"The purpose of every statement is to indicate the falsity of the previous one, only to await its own imminent demise."

+ Rupert Spira

MISCELLANEOUS NOTES FOR THIS WEEK

January 26th, 30__

+ One already Knowingly Knows the Known and the Unknown.

+ You yourself hold the keys to your own cell.

    When you feel confined, just step out.

+ Intent is everything.

    Whatever you direct your energy towards will reflect in your thoughts, your words, your actions, your interactions, and in your overall environment.

    Everything is energy and reflection, make sure your own vibrations are as harmonious as you want them reflected towards you.

January 27th, 30___

\+ The philosophy of the West will take one to the apex of the Intellect.

The wisdom of the East will take one to the depths of the Heart.

Learn both and then move on.

\+ Everything is, ultimately, derivative.

REMOVING CREATIVITY'S CURTAINS

January 29th, 30__

+ Why do we block ourselves from creating and expressing our greatest creative potential in this Lifetime?

What are the typical obstacles?

One obstacle that primarily comes to mind is our contemporary preoccupation for attaining fame and fortune.

There's this undercurrent of fear-thinking where we believe that there are all these great artists and celebrities "out there" constantly creating things that are thus released to the public and can't be matched by anyone who's not of equal and/or similar status.

This sort of thinking then hinders one from creating their own Art, as if one could never create something as "immense" or "grand" as that celebrity or well-regarded artist.

Ask yourself: *How did these "icons" get to where they are now?*

Were they not in a similar position you find yourself in now?

Has their every creation since birth been a masterpiece, and dually shared with the public?

Another common phenomenon in regards to blocking our creativity can come from studying and appreciating timeless works of Art, along with their respective artists.

Whether it's Michelangelo's precision, Da Vinci's versatility, Rodin's dexterity, or Shakespeare's poetic mastery, there is a grand and subtle trap.

It is a nuanced trap that many are caught by:

And the trap is this:

Not being able to create, and fully share your Art with the world until you consume enough historical and artistic knowledge of these timeless works of Art.

You deliberately stall your own creations because you feel like you can't compete with all these Art masters, leaving you with the natural drive to study them until you're "learned enough" to create something like them.

Thus, ensnaring yourself even further into the trap.

Instead, we must investigate and remind ourselves *why* we study Others.

Let's start with myself, why do I personally study Others?

- I study Others to free myself of any presently held, and possibly misinformed beliefs.

- I study Others because it's a way to experience perspectives and styles that I haven't yet considered before, and might use as inspiration to fuse into my own style.

- I study Others who have had similar experience(s), and/or interest(s) as me, to see what cool stuff they've discovered.
- I study Others to free myself of any presently held, self-imposed limitations, specifically including: what, why, and how I create.

Of course, we all like to create these stories in our head telling ourselves that we can't create, and/or share our creation(s) with the public, until we've studied enough,

Or whenever we "feel the time is right,"

Or whenever we "feel good enough,"

Or whenever we have "a solid enough portfolio" to release on some magical day....

But guess what bud?

The time to create is Now.

The time to share is Now.

You are a person with your own worthwhile experiences and unique inclinations waiting to be expressed with the world.

Now go for it.

Postscriptum:

To be as clear as I can, this isn't in any way, to dismiss and/or subvert these artistic masters and their respective masterpieces, but instead,

To reveal why we should study these timeless works of Art with balance and purpose.

Check the intent with which you use the precious time of your Life when studying and experiencing Others and their Art.

Study, but do it with purpose.

MASTER WY ON ART

January 30th, 30__

Miro: Master, what do you think Art is?

And what should it ultimately aim to do?

(*silence*)

Master Wy: What is Art?

Art.

Art.

(*silence*)

Art, I feel, is a euphemism for the freest kind of religion,

An eccentric and iconoclastic medium that attempts to describe and express this Whole Mystery, being Life.

This Mystery of Life continuously grants us this Intangible Energy we process with our physical and mental organisms, which then commingles with our own experiences, memories, thoughts, and ideas creating a physical manifestation that is birthed into our physical world.

This Mysterious Energy that is freely gifted to us—and *that* which flows through our fragile veins—transforms itself into a creative act that adds a whole new form to this Mystery.

In essence, we continuously add to our own individual and collective experience by our every act, word, and thought expressed,

An eternal recurrence of Creative Energy if you will.

This all then ruthlessly begs the time-worn question:

What should Art ultimately aim to do?

And I say to you:

I don't know.

All we are in this world are instruments to this Mysterious Melody that plays Itself.

> "The work of art is to dominate the spectator:
> the spectator is not to dominate the work of art.
> The spectator is to be receptive.
> He is to be the violin on which the master is to play.
> And the more completely he can suppress his own silly views,
> his own foolish prejudices, his own absurd ideas of what Art
> should be, or should not be, the more likely he is to understand
> and appreciate the work of art in question."
>
> + Oscar Wilde

The biggest trouble comes when we think we're the creators creating, when really, it is this Mysterious Energy flowing through us that reshapes Itself,

Transforming Itself into new forms playing with Its Own Recycled Energy.

Now, this isn't to say that we are completely off the hook in the creation process.

We co-create, and we co-create with intention.

When Inspiration comes through us, whether through Intuition, The Muses, God, our nervous system or whatever you might believe in,

It arrives in a certain packaging that is raw and untouched.

When one attempts to take that information and create it into existence, one inevitably interprets it.

High Art then, can be presumed, is the lowest diluted form of the Original Information given.

Low Art, can be presumed, is the highest diluted form of the Original Information given.

Low Art is when one excessively distorts the Original Information given, takes complete credit for the creation, and gets defensive when someone doesn't like the work.
It is ego-driven, narrow-minded, and shallow.

Conversely, High Art heals. It conveys a complex, yet simple understanding of one's self and one's World. It helps one, and Others, move from a lower understanding to a higher one aiding evolution in a sincere and serendipitous fashion.

High Art elevates one's self, and one's fellow man, by evoking feelings of: awe, bliss, euphoria, discomfort, anger, rage, inspiration, humor, nostalgia, love and/or any feelings that touch us and remind us of our Deepest of Depths.

Art should ultimately create a sense of union by harmonizing opposites and inspiring a deep sense of awe that is both palpable and equanimous with the Mystery that surrounds us —that is within us.

In its final analysis, everything is Art:

Every experience, feeling, thought, object, moment, word, situation, person, place, and thing is Art.

"The role of the artist is to transmit to humanity the deepest experience of reality. Art is remembrance. It is love. It is like a sword that distinguishes between appearances and reality, or a cradle that reminds us of home."

+ Rupert Spira

CHAPTER
417 Hz

Savoir's Notebook: Terrarum Orbis Tabula

ON WRITING: PART I

March 3rd, 30__

+ Distractions.

    So elusive, so alluring, so seductive.

    Thoughts currently plague my Consciousness, of which I now plan to ejaculate on this page and thoroughly unfetter myself.

    Not enough credit is given to paper—to trees.

    We tend to forget the weight placed on these looseleaf descendants that we entrust to hold our most sensitive thoughts, desires, and projections.

    Therefore, I have decided to take this small sliver of timelessness to act as humanity's temporary spokesman in thanking Nature, who has provided for us for years beyond measure.

    (silence)

    Thank you.

    (silence)

    Now, let us begin with our first enquiry into Existence:

What is writing for?

I don't know and I won't pretend to know.

There is no one answer that will satisfy you or I.

Writing is unique to each individual and I can only speak for myself.

Now, a couple answers reveal themselves when I contemplate the question: *What is writing for me?*

- Writing is a way to share myself with myself.

- Writing is a way to share myself with Others.

- Writing is a way to empty my mind.

- Writing is a way to fill my mind.

- Writing is a way to physically record Formless Inspiration into Form that spontaneously appears in my being.

- Writing is a way to put my believed-to-be-self's thoughts on paper, attempting to see them for what they truly are.

- Writing is a way to reveal appearances of Something Greater.

Never confine your writing style, nor your content to what you've been told is appropriate before.

Write what you want to.

Write what you need to.

"I write the way I want to, and that's the way it's going to be; the rest can do what they like…"

+ Søren Kierkegaard

MISCONSTRUING THE CONSTRUING

March 6th, 30__

+ I don't want to commit to any of these words, but I've realized one doesn't have to feel like they're committing to anything.

Rather, one can use words as tools—as bridges to express a Greater Reality.

We all have this potential to create.

It isn't just privy to a few "gifted" anomalies.

People will continue to read books, and ideas will continue to flow.

Why not participate in this process and communicate with Others through this beautiful medium of writing?

A form of communication where we don't necessarily meet face-to-face, but *being*-to-*being*.

We aren't aware of our telepathy, *just yet*, but writing and reading are a close second.

Ideas will *always* be misconstrued, leading to perpetual disappointment, yet that too must be transcended.

As long as we live in this dual world of concepts and ideas, the misconstruing will inescapably continue, so with this, we must fearlessly go *beyond* all concepts, ideas, and constructs of any sort.

FATHER: "But all the trouble is there, in words. We all have within us a world of things, each of us our own special world made of these things. Now how can we understand each other if I use words for these things that have meanings and values particular to my special world, while whoever hears my words relate them to meanings and values particular to his special world? We think we understand each other, but we never do."

+ Luigi Pirandello, *Six Characters in Search of an Author*

AESTHETIC VALIDATIONS

March 8th, 30__

+ Why do most of us feel that we need to be validated for what we say and do?

Why can't our actions be done for their own sake?

Do we really need Another's pair of eyes to see them, and Another's mouth to say that they're okay to do?

Are we looking for our parent's validation in some way? Our friends' validation?

Do we see them in our thoughts? In our actions? In our decision-making processes?

Have we carried this behavior from our childhood years when we needed to appease our parents and their levels of acceptance?

* * *

Why aren't we more self-reliant and confident in our selves and in our styles?

It feels as if there's this underlying fear we carry day-after-day, that we're going to be exposed as frauds at some point.

This kind of nuanced fear that someone will say that our style —our way of doing things—isn't the "right" way, and thus exposing us as non-genuine to Others in our environment.

Well…are we, indeed, frauds?

I don't know, *again*.

Yet, what I do seem to know is that the Non-Fraud is He, or She, who needs no validation from Others.

The Non-Fraud is She, or He, who trusts in their own ideas and follows them until it serves them no longer.

"Only that personality is mature who absorbs truth and makes it his own…"

+ Søren Kierkegaard

Your style is *your own* style.

Express it fully, without guilt, and with the utmost sincerity you are capable of.

Whatever you express, you profess.

Let go of what Others will think.

Whichever style you choose carries the implication that this is the highest style you believe to be best for you in this precise moment.

So, be careful when commenting, criticizing, and/or talking about Other's styles in any medium.

And why's that?

Because their style, the one you're currently judging, is the highest style they currently wish to express with their world.

It is the foundation of their current reality and you're the current asshole attempting to tear it down.

"Public opinion is a weak tyrant compared with our own private opinion. What a man thinks of himself, that it is which determines, or rather indicates, his fate."

+ Henry David Thoreau, *Walden*

ON WRITING: PART II

March 9th, 30__

+ Why else do I write?

    - To say what I don't think I can say in public?

    - To find relief in using aesthetically mature words that allows me to come closer in describing how I actually feel about something than ordinary conversation allows?

    - To show how much knowledge I think I possess?

    - To finally express something that only I and this piece of paper will be able to understand together?

"What can be said at all can be said clearly,
and what we cannot talk about we must pass over in silence."

+ Ludwig Wittgenstein, *Tractatus Logico-Philosophicus*

FAME & FORTUNE

March 12th, 30__

"Our life, said Pythagoras, is like the vast throng assembled for the Olympic Games: some use their bodies there to win fame from the contests; others come to trade, to make a profit; still others—and they are by no means the worst—seek no other gain than to be spectators, seeing how everything is done and why; they watch how other men live so that they can judge and regulate their own lives."

+ Michel de Montaigne

+ There's this underlying motif in my thoughts, projects, and actions that I've been intimately observant of and now inclined to share as clear and articulate as this pen and paper allow so.

This motif isn't exclusive to our present era, but one which is praised among all others:

The desire to be rich, famous, and well-regarded in the world.

Who doesn't want these things, right?

Well, Taoist Sages Lao-Tzu and Chuang Tzu probably wouldn't.

> "Do not race after riches;
> do not risk your life for success,
> or you will let slip the Heaven within you."

+ Chuang Tzu

> "What good is it to spend your life accumulating material things? It isn't in keeping with the Tao. What benefit in conforming your behavior to someone's conventions? It violates your nature and dissipates your energy. Why separate your spiritual life and your practical life? To an integral being, there is no such distinction. Live simply and virtuously, true to your nature, drawing no line between what is spiritual and what is not. Ignore time. Relinquish ideas and concepts. Embrace the Oneness."
>
> + Lao Tzu, *Hua Hu Ching*

Supposedly, the man of Tao isn't concerned with lofty ideals of fame and glamour, well-aware of the dangers of vanity and the surplus of riches, and adroitly versed in the true luxury of knowing one's most Intimate Identity.

That's all nice and dandy conceptually, but at the same time I have to keep reminding myself that I gotta be easy with myself knowing that the society I live in, approbates and glorifies fame to the *nth* degree.

We are constantly being fed these ideals of fame and wealth whether subliminally or directly.

They're all around us to condition our minds that being rich and famous is the highest of human achievements,

That one hasn't *truly* lived until one has achieved these things,

That one hasn't contributed enough to society to be worthy of possessing these things.

We are continuously bombarded with these inferiority complexes that our system registers and adds into its framework.

Thus, those without at least a partial awareness of this societal phenomenon are then conditioned with these borrowed ideals, embedded deeply within their system, coloring their every thought and action.

It should then be appropriate to say that these thoughts and actions, bred out of confusion, spread to create further confusion.

These ideals of fame and fortune appeal to our body's innate tendencies of wanting connection, security, happiness, and power.

We are constantly looking for these things in foolhardy ways, including, money and one's status in society.

Now, of course, it must be noted that there isn't *anything* inherently wrong with fame and fortune, only one's thoughts and intentions associated with them.

As Oscar Wilde notes in his essay "The Soul of Man Under Socialism":

> "There is only one class in the community that thinks more about money than the rich, and that is the poor."

Fame and fortune are necessary externals for us.

They allow us to strive for greatness, for perfection, for *beyond*.

They allow us abundance: financially, socially, and creatively.

They remind us of our Inherent Freedom in an external fashion.

They allow us to experience some of the highest pleasures and feelings of external security Life has to offer us.

When fame and/or fortune are sought and used with pure and uplifting intentions for one's self and one's neighbor (however this might look like), they are then necessary and instrumental.

When fame and/or fortune are sought for malicious intentions, as if to incur harm to one's self, and/or to one's neighbor, then one could begin speculating on their superfluousness and danger.

> "The industry for the making of money is also very demoralizing. In a community like ours, where property confers immense distinction, social position, honour, respect, titles, and other pleasant things of the kind, man, being naturally ambitious, makes it his aim to accumulate this property, and goes on wearily and tediously accumulating it long after he has got far more than he wants, or can use, or enjoy, or perhaps even know of."
>
> + Oscar Wilde

If we take a quick peek into history—and even at our current world—we can clearly see the injurious effects of the malicious intentions for power, money, and social acceptance, mostly through religious and political con games.

One group, and/or a collusion of a few groups, suppress all other interests in order to expound their philosophy and project it on to the masses.

Once power is "secured," even those within the group will begin concocting ways to take out those within their own group.

And the cycle inevitably perpetuates.

Regardless of the case, deep down, deep deep down, *we must* tap into our bodies, make friends with our aliveness—our simple existingness—and allow this familiar feeling of *just being*, to permeate, moment after moment after moment.

This is the Truest Wealth there is.

This is all there is.

THE BELIEVED-TO-BE-SELF

March 15th, 30__

+ It seems we've forgotten that we have a choice when it comes to our internal sphere and its movements.

Namely: our thoughts and their ongoing processes, moment after moment after moment.

We have been conditioned by Others, and ourselves, to identify with this steady stream of thoughts in which the believed-to-be-self—the ego—is continuously discriminating, judging, and evaluating as if it's clocked in and getting paid by the second.

In economical terms, whenever a thought passes by and it elicits a reaction out of you—whether attracting or repulsing you—you are inadvertently giving the believed-to-be-self power and *existence*. The believed-to-be-self profits whenever you identify with any of its fabricated thoughts and stories, further increasing its stock price and *existence* as a company.

The believed-to-be-self thrives off one's lack of attention.

What can one do you immediately ask yourself?

As a plethora of spiritual masters have gently suggested:

Be aware of The Subtle Voice which possesses a different quality to the one the believed-to-be-self verbalizes.

Be aware of The Subtle Feeling which possesses a different quality to the one the believed-to-be-self anxiously feeds.

One can practice this as the Sages of Hinduism, Zen Buddhism, Sufism, Christian mysticism, Jewish mysticism, and any other *-ism*/non-*ism* would tell us:

Keep catching your Attention when it attempts to identify its identity with any fabricated thoughts and related stories concocted by a non-existent believed-to-be-self.

Disidentify your sense of identity from them. Know that you do not actually share the limited nature of these temporary thoughts and feelings.

Your attention is dim from lack of practice and years of habitual identifying with these thoughts and feelings; therefore, one is prone to keep "going back to sleep" as the mystic Gurdjieff claims.

Keep coming out of this "sleep" (lack of attention) by investigating who the believed-to-be-self actually is and where it lives.

Who's the one thinking all these thoughts?

Is "the thinker" of thoughts *really* you? Is it your *actual* identity?

If you do believe your identity is "the thinker" of thoughts, then riddle me this one:

Who is the one watching the thinker think these thoughts?

IMPRESSIONS FROM A MONTH SPENT WITH MASTER WY

March 30th, 30__

- The Fundamentals of Life:

    - This Moment (Experiencing)

    - This Body (In which Experiencing is happening, thoughts, sensations, and emotions)

    - Energy-Space (The stuff in which Experience and our bodies are made of)

    - Attention (The thing that is *aware* of all of this happening)

- The quality of one's Attention determines the quality of one's experience.

- The main reactions my body produces, are the main reactions my thoughts produce.

    The main reactions my thoughts produce, are the main reactions my world produces.

- Life is a playground to experience and play with Attention.

+ Awakening, or spiritual awakening, if you will, is none other than a fashionable name we use to describe a significant shift of Attention.

+ Let go of *that person* who thinks *that person* is actually *a person*.

+ Beliefs can be seen as subtle defense mechanisms created from past experiences we didn't know how to properly cope with before, as well as being subtle defense mechanisms we use to protect us from re-experiencing similar, overwhelming situations in the future.

+ When does thinking of the past happen? Now.

   When does thinking of the future happen? Now.

   When does thinking of the present happen? Now.

+ "My" only job on this Earth is:

   To fully be.

   This means: fully settling into my body as the recognition of Awareness permeating everywhere, my every cell dancing with spaciousness, allowing this Awareness to do everything without any feeling of "my" doing. *Just being.* This is the highest activity one can perform as a human *being*. Every other activity points to this one.

   You can let go now.

"The question of existence never gets straightened out except through existing itself."

+ Martin Heidegger

+ **Meditation**: the experience of Space, Attention, and the body harmonizing.

+ If someone feels resistance to meditate, it's because meditation is nothing more than an experience of dying to *who you think you are*.

    It is an arduous process that includes continuously watching any pain, feelings, and old beliefs stored within you, rise to the surface, and transmute with grace, passivity, and understanding.

    Instead of seeing the believed-to-be-self as a constant hindrance, attempt to see it as a teacher.

    Observe what it has to show you: the points where you still react, the triggers of the world, the triggers from those around you, the false stories, feelings, and sensations you keep believing in.

    Give them all space to be released and reconciled within the body.

"All things will follow you when their life is done."

+ Lucretius

"Every time the mind complains, supplicates, pleads, prods, or demands, we simply register the message and then continue with whatever we were doing before being interrupted. This reins in the mind and reconditions our internal process by not reacting as we normally do. The more we delay our response to these signals, the less compelling they seem to be. This is the road to mastering inner silence."

+ David A. Cooper

+ Ultimately, these words are for myself.

They might come off as absolute truths, but I mean no harm.

These words are just symbols pointing to intangible forms:

The intangible forms of my internal movements.

Words are the physical representations of my internal movements dancing,

Dancing to express Reality,

And not just for my own eyes, but for the eyes of All.

Others give us meaning.

Others give us purpose.

CHAPTER
528 Hz

Wissen's Notepad

April 3rd, 30__

+ Look at this little guy, writing in his little green 80-page notepad like he thinks he's someone at all.

The more he writes, the more he's attempting to justify the seemingly endless repetition of butter-glazed moments eluding his grasp.

This little guy nursing his little black coffee, with its little brown beans originating somewhere in the heart of Colombia, looks for a theme and purpose for this excuse of an essay.

This little guy is me, or so "I" think so.

I speak to myself and myself alone.

My final speech on Earth is every sentence, word, letter, and silence.

I don't know which one will be my last, so they're all significant.

There was a baby sitting next to me a couple minutes ago sporting a sheep costume.

That was the most significant thing a few moments ago.

Now it's gone.

This little pen is lifted from its sojourn and this little guy recovers from a little strain in his little right hand.

How can I be as honest as possible with you?

How can I be as honest as possible with myself?

How can I entertain you?

How can I entertain myself?

Are we constantly performing for each other?

Are we constantly performing for ourselves?

How's my acting doing so far?

Is this ruse worth keeping up?

Should I pretend this now stale, warmified dark mahogany liquid we properly label: coffee, still tastes as great as it did a couple sips ago?

I guess this is why people use containers to prolong those first ethereal sips of hot java.

Hot Java. Hot Java. Hot Java.

Why do we pretend with one another?

Is it all a friendly disguise to buy time to see where a person truly stands?

To see what character their character is characterized by?

To try to figure out what their understanding of Life is compared to ours?

To see if they're a threat to us or not?

How primitive that is, still thinking about Others as threats to one's status, level of intelligence, and/or survival.

How have we not resolved these problems in our "modern" age?

Are these constant preoccupations—however subtle or palpable they are—the fault of our contemporary systems of economics? Education? Government? Genetics?

The answer cannot be boiled down to one thing.

Or could it…?

"I" doesn't know, nor can ever know.

It can only keep up this game, this ruse it loves playing:

*Attaching its sense of permanence and importance to whatever it can get its meaty hands on, veiling **what is**.*

What is *is* what is and will won't be for the remainder of what is' is.

LORD KRISHNA: "Nothing of nonbeing comes to be,
nor does being cease to exist;
the boundary between these two
is seen by men who see reality.

Indestructible is the presence
that pervades all this;
no one can destroy
this unchanging reality."

+ *The Bhagavad-Gita*

TODAY'S DIALOGUE WITH MASTER WY

April 4th, 30__

Wissen: Master, can you tell me the best way to start one's day?

(*silence*)

Master Wy: (*clears throat*)

There is no one "best" way for everyone Wissen.

There is no one prescription for all to follow.

There are only "best" ways to start the day for yourself and that's it.

Wissen: Alright, well I'm down with that.

(*silence*)

MasterWy: I consider ourselves part of a Sequence,

A Sequence with a beginning, middle, and an end of an even Grander Sequence.

(*silence*)

Likewise, each day is a Sequence, in which energy seemingly comes and goes.

We are graciously supplied energy for each day, and then given the opportunity to use it and direct it in whichever manner appropriate to our personal dispositions and current Life circumstances.

We assume we wake up as the same person everyday,

When, *really*, we can choose to be someone different.

If we assume that we're the same exact person, day after monotonous day, Life loses its Inherent Rawness, its Sparkle, its Luminescence.

You help shape your own Life by how you manage your physical and mental energy.

What are you focusing on most of the time? Half of the time? 1/6th of time?

(*silence*)

Wissen: Maybe a tad bit more of specificity Master, like day-to-day activities and such?

Master Wy: I wake up early.

I shower my organs with water, inside and out.

I brush my teeth, I floss.

I spend time outside, connect with Mother Earth in some way.

But the most important thing I do, the *most important thing I do every single day,* is remind myself of my transience, my limited time here on Earth, and what it is I need to do before time's up, which…

Usually entails things I need to appreciate and be more grateful for.

Wissen: I see. (*pause*)

So, that's it? That's your every morning?

Master Wy: (*smiling*) I also don't mind a nice, cold glass of orange juice.

Wissen: (*laughs*)

Master Wy: The most important aspect of one's day is to dedicate your energy to things you enjoy doing.

It is a new day to learn, to progress, to share unforgettably mundane and mystical experiences with Others also living on this exquisite planet.

As our Transcendentalist friend Henry David Thoreau writes in his masterpiece *Walden*:

> "It is something to be able to paint a particular picture,
> or to carve a statue, and so to make a few objects beautiful;
> but it is far more glorious to carve and paint the very
> atmosphere and medium through which we look,
> which morally we can do.
> To affect the quality of the day, that is the highest of arts."

Play with the scenes Life continuously gives you.

In the end, it is your own Masterpiece to craft and live out.

(*silence*)

Wissen: (*bowing*) Thank you Master.

(*silence*)

Master Wy: Let's go for a walk.

BY THE RIVER

(*silence*)

Wissen: Master, can you please speak to me of—

Master Wy:

The Sun's Spotlight.

On Dark Green Canopy.

Untouched.

(*silence*)

Wissen: Master, that was refreshing and all, but what does that have to do with—

Master Wy: That's just how it happened to happen Wissen. Give it a whack.

Wissen: (*thinking*)

The silent wind affects, yet shies.

It wants to make its Presence known, yet hides behind the Veil.

O! Brave New Wind!

Blow me away until I am no more.

(silence)

Master Wy: Continue with your inquiry.

Wissen: The body—our body—how does the ideal relationship to it look like?

(silence)

Master Wy: The body.

I'm glad you asked this question Wissen.

Yes, the body is more than a temple, as they say.

It is a sanctuary.

Strive to be aware of everything, *everything,* that you put inside of your body, because it will inevitably become you in some way.

(silence)

Strive to feel your body's cellular movements and its flowing, pulsing energy moving throughout moment after moment.

Let the sense of Awareness travel through every pour and passage of your body.

Strive to feel the multi-sensorial experience that you normally evade feeling moment after moment.

This dynamic helps take attention away from the mind, and a non-existent believed-to-be-self creating nonsense after nonsense, story after story.

The body's functioning and one's knowledge of its functioning is of the utmost importance.

It is the only way we can experience Life in its Completeness.

The cells and its memories are where almost everything originates from, not your mind.

Yet, we seem to only occupy the upper half of our bodies on a day-to-day basis because we think thinking is apparently happening up there.

We seem to only recognize our feet and the rest of the body when they are directly pointed out, or involved more than usual in an activity.

Many teachings nowadays either undermine the body, demonize it, and/or encourage us to disembody completely.

But, this is not the way.

Stray away from any of these teachings that speak ill of the body; this is all a subtle technique to push away Life instead of embracing it in its Fullness, in its Entirety.

The body is the vehicle to experience and express who we actually are.

In short, *let Life in*, include the Awareness of your entire body moment after moment after moment.

Sensations, constricting movements, nervous system holding patterns, thoughts, feelings, emotions, *embrace them all, let them melt away on their own by being the spaciousness of your body, moment after moment after moment.*

Wissen: Mmm. So, you're saying the body is a sanctuary, and I understood everything you just said Master, and I fully agree,

But can't it also be a prison as well?

Master Wy: Mmhm. Very precocious of you Wissen.

Yes, yes it can.

The prison-body phenomenon is akin to someone thinking their Halloween costume, on Halloween, is their real and ultimate identity for all other days of the year.

A garment—*only to be worn temporarily*—is mistaken to be their real identity, when really, it is only a costume—an appearance serving a temporary purpose.

(*silence*)

Wissen: Master, I have another question—and I'm sorry for asking all these questions, but I—

Master Wy: Stop. Why are you sorry?

Wissen: I—I don't know, it's just a habit of saying I guess, along with some guilt for asking you all these questions…

Master Wy: Wissen, don't waste your time with guilt, it will get you nowhere worthwhile. You are here for a month studying with me, use it wisely.

Wissen: I will.

Master Wy: Wissen, remember this clearly:

My answers will mean very little to you.

Wissen: But—but, they mean more than you think Master.

Master Wy: Yes, yes, they're important on one level, yet you will have to unlearn all of this at some point and come up with answers of your own.

Borrowed knowledge, advice, they're cheap.

(silence)

CHAPTER
639 Hz

Capire's Notebook of Impromptu Insights Lying Around

June 7th, 30__

+ Whether in public, or in private, why do we get filled with feelings of worry and anxiety about what Others are thinking about us?

How we look, what we do, what we say.

This can all fit under the umbrella term: "considering" in which, I believe, the mystic George Gurdjieff first coined.

We are constantly plagued with a secret worry that Another's believed-to-be-self (ego) won't like our believed-to-be-self (ego),

That their mask won't approve of our mask, that their mask won't want to connect with our mask.

So with this, naturally, we "consider" Others in our thoughts and in our actions,

Thus, influencing our present and future thoughts as to what we think Other's would like us to do so that they can finally accept and connect with us.

Why are we even trying to fulfill Other's believed-to-be-self's?

What do we have to prove to them and why?

What will this necessarily do for us?

Are we all just well-functioning schizophrenics disguising our condition with all these word games, distractions, and needless running around we do?

Are we so deep in our delusions that we have forgotten what truly lies deeper?

A DAY AT A FUNERAL HOME

June 8th, 30__

+ Idle, yet in motion.
  Laughs and chatter fill the space with purpose.

  Remembrance of things past and present
  Make themselves known with pristine clarity.

  "Asi es la vida mija."
  "Todos nos vamos algun dia."
  "Fuerza hijo, fuerza."

  These are the quips and tricks that prevail tonight's
  introductory remarks among loved ones.

  And I'm currently in The Midst of It All.

  I am their warm embraces.

  I am their mourning conversations.

  I am their softened eye gazes.

  I am their prayers muttered under warm breath.

  I am the register book signed with intent.

  I am the square-cut laminated cards read and carefully put into polyester chest pockets.

  I am the screen and the projector showing memories cherished too late.

I am the flowers.

I am the urn and the delicate obsidian ash moving closer to union with the sea.

I am the Funeral's Service Assistant.

I am Death.

June 9th, 30__

+ Everybody who knew you while you were alive will remember you for *something* when you leave your body.

  It could be one thing, it could be two, it could be a couple more.

  But nonetheless, we all attach certain memories, experiences, and concepts onto Others.

  These will all amalgamate to create the filters that will influence our mourning processes and decide how we'll carry the memories of our loved ones onward.

  The essential question to ask yourself here is:

  How do I want to be remembered?

SURELY

June 12th, 30__

+ The seeming sureties of one's Life seem surely for a while,

That is, until they dissolve and fresh new sureties take their place.

Surely, you realize the trials and tribulations, and the lies that we lead, begin with a seed.

They behaved purely, despite the "surely" foretold promise of deceit.

It was all a story, a story's story telling a story.

I can assure you living a spiritually insured life allures a comforting darkness.

+ A poem by 4 people in a room

"The digression is a strategy for putting off the ending,
a multiplying of time within the work,
a perpetual evasion or flight.
Flight from what? From death, of course…"

+ Italo Calvino, *Six Memos for the Next Millennium*

TRANSCRIPT OF PENULTIMATE DISCOURSE

June 30th, 30__

Capire: Master, I've seen that many times through conversation with Another, I find myself with readymade answers anxiously waiting to come out, usually at the expense of my attention on what the other person is saying.

How can I be a better conversationalist?

Master Wy: It sounds like you answered your own question Capire.

Capire: Yea, maybe, but I feel there's something else missing.

Conversations occupy such a big part of my Life, and I'd like to rectify this issue of mine as soon as possible.

I'd love to hear your thoughts on the topic Master.

(silence)

Master Wy: *(takes a sip of tea)*

Number 1: Constantly experiment.

(silence)

To be a great conversationalist, one must be a great listener.

Number 2: One must rid their own self of any pre-constructed ideas about the Other person, their words, and the overall situation.

Fully *be* with someone when you're *with* someone.

Are you *actually* listening to them *or* are you listening to your own mind's agenda-laced ramblings?

(*silence*)

Number 3: Feel your body, both inside and out.

Know what your body is doing at all moments.

Are your movements purposeful or are they wasteful?

That individual is mature who moves with purpose, grace, and awareness in their every movement.

Capire: How about when speaking?

(*silence*)

Mastery Wy: Speak *what is* necessary.

Speak *when is* necessary.

Speak from Inspiration.

As Kahlil Gibran masterfully writes in *The Prophet*:

"…let the spirit in you move your lips and direct your tongue. Let the voice within your voice speak to the ear of his ear."

Capire: Mmm, that's a beautiful quote. So then, what should I do if someone isn't fully listening to me?

Master Wy: Then speak briefly.

Show them what true listening looks like.

Be the example you would want Others to exemplify,

As French philosopher and writer Jean-Paul Sartre also masterfully writes:

> "But in truth, one ought always to ask oneself what would happen if everyone did as one is doing…"

Capire: How about when I talk to girls, to women?

Master Wy: What about them?

Capire: How should I talk to them?

Master Wy: I'm guessing you mean "flirtatiously?"

Capire: Yeah…

Master Wy: Eradicate all preconceptions of how to relate to women in a flirtatious way.

Flirting comes naturally of its own accord and should never be forced.

Additionally, there should be minimal mental boundaries and/or anxiousness, between both of you whether in public or private.

Tell me, what is there to be anxious about?

You are both living on Earth.

You will both die at some point.

Treat them as your mirror.

Capire: What about my parents?

Master Wy: Well…(*clears throat*) I definitely wouldn't suggest trying to flirt with them.

Capire: No, no, no! (*laughing*)

I didn't mean it like that, I mean like how should I relate to my parents? They get me so frustrated sometimes, like there's an enormous gulf of misunderstanding between us.

(*silence*)

Master Wy: This is normal.

Begin by understanding thy mother & father.

Reflect on everything they have sacrificed, everything they have done to affect where you are now.

Work with wherever they are in their own development as they have duly done with you and your infantile capriciousness for years.

Capire: I know, I know, it's just so hard, even when knowing this consciously. I get triggered so easily by them.

(*silence*)

Master Wy: Who's triggering who?

Capire: *They* trigger *me*.

Master Wy: Really? How so?

Capire: I don't know, by doing and saying things that just get me mad sometimes.

Master Wy: Are they also responsible for how *you* react to what they say and do?

Capire: No…

Master Wy: Then, who's responsible for that?

Capire: I am.

Master Wy: And who's that?

Capire: Me?

Master Wy: Who's this "me?"

Capire: Capire! Who else?

Master Wy: Show him to me.

Capire: I'm right here Master.

Master Wy: Where? Where is Capire located?

Capire: I'm right here Master!

Master Wy: WHERE?!

Capire: HERE!

Master Wy: (*laughs*)

      (*silence*)

Too much has been said today.

Let us go outside and enjoy Nature's Free Symphony.

ASSORTED IMPRESSIONS FROM MASTERY WY'S DISCOURSES

+ Everything is necessary for Everything Else.

+ Life's continuous and intangible dialogue with us:

    "And then?

    Yes, and then?"

+ Tell yourself the stories that will let you live the greatest Life you can imagine.

    Create those narratives, feed them to yourself daily, and live from those foundations until you outgrow them and create new stories.

"Gradually it has become clear to me what every great philosophy so far has been: namely the personal confession of its author and a kind of involuntary and unconscious memoir."

+ Nietzsche, *Basic Writings of Nietzsche*

+ When debating with Others, keep reassessing exactly what you're both debating about.

   This is so because the essence of the debate can get lost in translation, which can lead to two or more topics being debated as the same topic.

   Notice the dual-paradox in all arguments, situations, and things.

   Define your definitions.

   Be clear, concise, and succinct with your questions and responses.

   > "If you wish to converse with me, define your terms."
   >
   > + Voltaire

+ The way music can instantly remind you of someone and inspire feelings from an experience you both went through together is Beyond the Utterable.

+ Sound connects us all together.

   And speaking is a form of singing.

   Make sure it's pleasurable for Other's ears.

+ There's a language behind the one we all speak.

   It's charmingly familiar and all that matters.

"I think we are always searching for something hidden or merely potential or hypothetical, following its traces whenever they appear on the surface."

+ Italo Calvino

Stop.

Feel your *whole* body.

Continue.

CHAPTER
741 Hz

Loro's Log

August 6th, 30__

+ Why do we go around pretending like we know exactly where we are?

  I am always enthralled by those willing to speak of this Grand Ruse.

  Does anybody else see what's going on?!

  Is anybody else witnessing this Endless Serendipity dripping from our each and every passing breath?!

  Is anybody else witnessing these movements of objects in standstill-motion?!

  Is anybody else catching on to this ongoing script improvised by a Transparent Bard?!

  IS ANYBODY ELSE SEEING THIS TOO?!

"We are turning in the same circle, ever therein confined."

+ Lucretius, *De Rerum Natura*

August 8th, 30__

+ Why do you think this was written?

Others are hiding in plain sight who Know.

At this point, my best bet is to do as Others did in the past who were as equally perplexed-in-awe by this Grand Ruse:

By writing down what's worth writing down.

And this is due to two reasons:

1) To serve as brief comfort for those who Know in this current epoch of time, including oneself,

And:

2) As a brief comfort for those in the future, fervently searching for Truth in their own contemporary present, and recorded version of the past.

"However, instead of ending his life, [Buckminster] Fuller decided (perhaps because of his deep conviction in the underlying unity and order of the universe, of which he knew himself to be an integral part) to live from then on *as if* he had died that night. Being dead, he wouldn't have to worry about how things worked out for himself personally and would be free to devote himself to living as a representative of the universe. The rest of his life would be a gift. Instead of living for himself, he would devote himself to asking, 'What is it on this planet [which he referred to as Spaceship Earth] that needs doing that I know something about, that probably won't happen unless I take responsibility for it?'"

+ Jon Kabat-Zinn, *Wherever You Go, There You Are*

August 9th, 30__

"The search for something permanent is one of the deepest of the instincts leading men to philosophy."

+ Bertrand Russell

+ Every philosophy, tradition, concept, and religion is necessary until it's not.

August 12th, 30__

+ Characters of any story are all synecdoches of mental states.

Better said: characters of any story are all anthropomorphized mental states.

The villain/the antagonist is usually portrayed with the most loathed aspects of the believed-to-be-self:
narcissism, greed, deception, lust, jealousy, pride, etc.

While, the hero is generally equipped with the most lauded aspects of human character: bravery, grit, wisdom, humility, perseverance, love, gratitude, etc.

This could be the essence of the quintessential "Hero's Journey" structure (popularized by Joseph Campbell):

First, the hero begins by desiring something, which naturally implies suffering of some sort,

The hero then acknowledges either the obstacle and/or villain blocking them from fulfilling this desire,

The hero then embarks on a journey that entails its own form of creative trials and tribulations, with the conclusion *usually* consisting of the hero fulfilling their original desire and transcending the villain.

I know, I know, that was an overly simplified and paraphrased version of Joseph Campbell's Hero's Journey structure but so what.

The way I'm currently choosing to interpret the Hero's Journey in my terms is like this:

The Hero = One's Inherent Awareness

The Villain = One's believed-to-be-self, one's ego, mental states of maya (illusion).

The Hero represents our Inherent Awareness as human beings, with the Villain being an aspect of the believed-to-be-self that calls to be transcended.

Thus, The Archetypal Life/Hero's Journey is this:

One's Inherent Awareness being liberated from the illusion of the believed-to-be-self and seemingly regaining unity with Itself.

"The quest for the self has always ended, and always will end, in a paradoxical dissatisfaction.
I don't say defeat."

+ Milan Kundera

"In devising a story, therefore, the first thing that comes to my mind is an image that for some reason strikes me as charged with meaning, even if I cannot formulate this meaning in discursive or conceptual terms. As soon as the image has become sufficiently clear in my mind, I set about developing it into a story; or better yet, it is the images themselves that develop their own implicit potentialities, the story they carry within them. Around each image others come into being, forming a field of analogies, symmetries, confrontations."

+ Italo Calvino

August 15th, 30__

- Leaders are those who show Others a higher level of Freedom not thought possible before.

  We all convey statements to Others and they in turn receive the message and interpret it from their unique level of Consciousness.

  Accept everyone from whichever level they're performing from.

  They're performing from the highest level they believe is possible, like your own self is.

  What's the point of this seeming hierarchical Realm of Understanding you ask?

  Well, where would the fun lie if everyone had the same level of Understanding?

  The Game would probably implode, or flourish.

  Too big of a gamble for The Big Guy Upstairs.

August 18th, 30__

+ Life is an ongoing play with an improvised script.

  Every scene is significant.

+ The measure of a concept's brilliance is in its ability to elevate various people's level of understanding simultaneously.

+ Stories are prime playgrounds for the expressions of Spirit to be played out.

+ Personal notebooks are platforms of creativity, the very foundation of our Muse's playground.

  It is a place to entertain, a place to lose one's "normal" self(s).

  It is a performance between you and you.

+ Ask yourself: *Through what mediums/platforms does my Muse move most effortlessly through me?*

August 21st, 30__

+ Financial wealth is the external manifestation of the utmost future security in one's survival and appeasement of the senses.

+ We exalt celebrities and the wealthy to such elevated heights because they are our daily reminders of a "lost" sort of abundance that we know we're allowed to have, a "lost" sort of freedom that we know we are.

+ Ask yourself: *If I were incredibly wealthy right now, what would I be doing? How would I spend my time on Earth?*

August 24th, 30__

+ All relationships of any kind are just a peeling of layers.

    Layer upon layer upon layer of each personality being shed with the center always being Love.

    Continuous peeling.

    Keep going deeper.

    Deeper.

    Deeper.

    The Nectar always tastes even sweeter.

+ Life is too interesting for so many formalities.

August 25th, 30__

+   All there is, is *this*.

August 26th, 30__

+ We all live our lives from the very highest knowledge and understanding we currently possess, which are absorbed from our most impactful experiences on Earth.

We subconsciously use our most impactful experiences on Earth as reference points in our daily lives to get back to the highest state we know.

For the artist, it's getting back to that space where Inspiration flows abundantly without reservation.

For the drug addict, it's getting back to the highest sensation of pleasure they have ever experienced.

For the Bhakti yogi, it's getting back to the highest feelings of Love and Well-Being that has ever graced their body.

All of these instances have a common golden thread and it is this:

Returning to the highest space one has ever been in, with the expectation of transcending and moving beyond it.

We *always* know there is Something Greater waiting for us.

"If we could capture a glimpse of the spiritual treasure which awaits us, nothing could restrain us from doing everything in our power to claim our Divine inheritance.
In that glimpse, we would realize that nothing in the transitory world could compare in any way to the experience of the love, freedom, and bliss that awaits us."

+ Shuddhaanandaa Brahmachari,
The Incredible Life of a Himalayan Yogi: The Times, Teachings and Life of Living Shiva: Baba Lokenath Brahmachari

CHAPTER
852 Hz

Perceber's Journal

QUACK

September 6th, 30__

+ "Quack."

The first word of this magnificent journal.

Being written and experienced by the intersection of
_____ & _____.

"I" sits here on this extremely uncomfortable metal park bench, pretending to write with the airs of a mystic scholar,

Pretending, sitting, and sipping his peppermint tea while cars whiz by to Source knows where.

"I" picks up his head in feeling intervals to make sure the Play is still Playing,

People walking and going all in their own beautiful/unbeautiful rhythms.

Has "I" conquered the Mystery of this Great Universe by parking himself on this incredibly inconvenient street bench, writing these silly lines that connect and separate themselves on cream-colored paper, all while observing the Play play on?

Looofidast is the answer.

Yet,

It's nice to pretend, to act.

That's what we're naturally doing anyways.

Pretending-acting-pretending-acting-pretending-acting.

Some just choose to cut through our societal formalities in a creative and playful way while pretending and acting,

While Others choose a more solemn route of pretending and acting, erroneously taking their body and personality as real and ultimate, causing misery for themselves and others around them.

The tragedy here is those in the latter category don't consciously realize that they're actually pretending and acting the whole time.

> "A fool thinks himself to be wise,
> but a wise man knows himself to be a fool."
>
> + William Shakespeare, *As You Like It*

ON EXPECTATION

September 8th, 30__

+ When one reveals a "new" piece of information about themselves and their relative place in the World, one naturally creates *expectations*.

These expectations are dressed in the form of thoughts and emotions—with an array of expectations to choose from in the beginning.

After a process of unique filtering, the mind then accommodates itself to the most suitable expectation in relation to:

The specific subject, one's interests and inclinations, one's personality, one's habitual mental tendencies, and one's habitual cellular patterns.

The expectation one chooses is the expectation one has chosen to replay the most within one's mind and body.

The more the expectation repeats itself—in the form of thoughts and emotions—the more one believes that's how things really are.

Hence, why our thoughts and emotions are akin to narcotics in distorting our projection of the Past, the Present, and the Future.

Most of us don't keep a conscious eye on our thoughts and emotions—at least not for stretched out periods of time—thus why we fail to understand our sporadic moods.

We fool ourselves with all this psychological and emotional masturbation that actually gets us nowhere.

We believe that these ideas, emotions, feelings, concepts, and theories are propelling us forward to some imagined destination where all of our problems will finally disappear forever.

Complete garbage.

When we realize nothing's working, we ask ourselves why things aren't working out the way we envisioned,

Leading us to blame either the internal and/or the external for our problems, when, really, it's neither's fault.

It's because of our quality of Attention.

ON THE PREMISE OF THE PREMISE'S PREMISE

September 9th, 30__

+ What is the premise to precede the following sub-premises?

Is the first premise of this epistle the foundation for all the following premises within the boundaries of this epistle?

Or is each sub-premise a premise within itself and only for its own sake?

Who's to say?

Can we just say both perspectives, put this pen down, and close this cartoony, 80-page, black-and-white composition notebook?

We could.

But, where does the fun lie in that?

Why don't I just keep writing down these questions to temporarily satisfy idle curiosities that really won't satisfy anything?

I'll just write it all down for the sake of my temporal well-being, while, possibly, soothing your temporal well-being as well.

What a relief when this phenomenon occurs:

When both spectator and artist intimately connect in an ethereal locus in the Labyrinth of Awareness.

Which leads me to impromptu and completely baseless conclusions:

What humans *think* humans truly crave:

Confirmation of our selves, our thoughts, and our unique perceptions and opinions of the world.

What we truly crave:

The person, thing, and/or concept that will best explain/express this Mystery of Life to us.

"When Wisdom has been profitless to me, and Philosophy barren, and the proverbs and phrases of those who have sought to give me consolation as dust and ashes in my mouth, the memory of that little lowly silent act of Love has unsealed for me all the wells of pity, made the desert blossom like a rose, and brought me out of the bitterness of lonely exile into harmony with the wounded, broken and great heart of the world."

+ Oscar Wilde, *De Profundis*

LECTURE TRANSCRIPT #3

September 12th, 30___

Perceber: Master, what do we crave?

Master Wy: Perceber, where is this question coming from?

Perceber: I don't know, I just feel like in some periods of my Life I'll be obsessed with something for however long, whether a couple months or whatever, and then I'll just move on to the next thing like nothing just happened…I feel that I lack some sort of consistency.

Master Wy: Why do you think that is?

Perceber: I don't know, maybe it's some sort of way I distract myself.

(silence)

Recently, it's been occurring to me—this feeling—as if we're all distracting ourselves somehow.

Master Wy: All of who?

Perceber: Human beings. *Us*.

Master Wy: So, you're speaking for *all* of humanity now? *All* of *us*?

Perceber: *(laughs)* Okay, I get it. But still, what are *most* of us distracting ourselves from?

Lack of meaning?

Lack of purpose?

Master Wy: Perceber! You nihilist! Leave now!

Perceber: No, no, I don't mean it like that Master.

Master Wy: Yes, then how?

Perceber: I mean it more like in the meaning of our meaninglessness.

It seems like we all come up with our own distraction(s) from truly living Life to its fullest potential,

And, the majority just end up copying one another,

And it all becomes this collectively sad attempt to fill this well-of-meaninglessness-and-emptiness with distractions.

(silence)

Television, work, movies, video games, social media, books, the news, friends, vacations, excuses, excuses, excuses from looking within.

We love creating and finding new stories—usually drama-filled—to give some sort of meaning to the current moment for oh so long, until one is back baby,

Face-to-face with the Substratum of Emptiness once again.

Then again—scared—we immediately search for the nearest, entertaining, and most convenient distraction to look away from this Penetrating Emptiness all around and within us.

Why?

Is it to lessen its intensity?

To numb one's self from feeling completely worthless?

To give oneself the illusion that one is actually *something*.

Why?
>   (*silence*)

Master Wy: Perceber, you have believed the greatest lie a human being could believe in this Lifetime.

A lie that was only meant to be used for practicality is the *root source* of all the unpracticality known to man.

And the lie is this:

Believing that you are someone.

ON PERVADING EMPTINESS

September 15th, 30__

> WINNIE: "What is one to do (*Head down. Do*)?
> All day long. (*Pause. Do.*)
> Day after day."

+ Samuel Beckett, *Happy Days*

+ When in The Midst of It All, when all Hell is breaking and shaking loose,

No philosopher, mystic, writer, priest, nor artist will be able to pull you out of the shitstorm you're currently in.

Sure, a certain phrase or poetically-placed words in harmonious succession will at best give one brief relief from suffering, but only for so long.

When in The Midst of It All you should—

(*silence*)

I don't know okay—I just don't…

And if someone pretends to know, and/or understand, what happens when in The Midst of it All,

Slap them with the nearest piece of tilapia you can find.

The process goes something like this:

(Get that tilapia ready.)

You begin with a feeling of internal space that you currently inhabit and label with some sort of meaning,

This space is your mind, along with the corresponding thoughts you have chosen to believe and carry forward to create the perception of your current world.

Then, a feeling that can best be described as an Emptiness begins to creep in.

This Emptiness can be characterized as a feeling that repeats a similar sentence over and over again, underlying your every thought, with a nonchalant urgency:

"What is the meaning of my existence?"

"What is the meaning of my existence?"

"What is the meaning of my existence?"

Followed by a subsequent question:

"Is there even meaning?"

"Is there even meaning?

Is there even…?"

Is there?

I don't know.

Yet, what I *can* say based on my encounters with Emptiness is this:

This Emptiness makes you feel as if your perception has shed pounds of distractions and what's left is a clearer picture of Reality staring Itself in the Face.

It's as if Perceber-the-personality, has been shed, chopped, and screwed into microscopic pieces of air sidestepping center stage and leaving room for the mirror downstage to be seen by the audience itself.

Inherent Emptiness everywhere I look.

Formless, Boundary-less, Without Outline.

Nothingness.

How can one picture nothingness?

Here:

I do not exist.

This is all One Formless Space in various forms expressing Itself.

The Center. The Centerless Center. You are the Center.

Find the Center.

You think you can catch It, and then you realize It's impossible to track, grasp, or understand.

Who's trying to catch It?

Who's trying to catch who?

Demolish all the story lines you think you're on right now.

And now demolish them in this moment.

And now in this one too.

Continuous demolishing.

(silence)

Irrespectively, I recognize that Emptiness cannot harm Emptiness in any way,

I recognize that *this* is all part of the experience,

And I honor It all for what It's all worth.

"To praise is to praise how one surrenders to the emptiness."

+ Rumi, "Buoyancy"

"Die, and be quiet.
Quietness is the surest sign that you've died.
Your old life was a frantic running from silence."

+ Rumi, "Quietness"

September 17th, 30__

+ How does one live their Life after knowing that everyone and everything is made of the Same Substance?

> LORD KRISHNA: "I am the taste in water, Arjuna
> the light in the moon and sun,
> OM resonant in all sacred lore,
> the sound in space, valor in men."
>
> + *The Bhagavad-Gita*

ON RELIEVING SUFFERING

September 18th, 30__

+ From a relative point-of-view, every interaction with Another Being is an opportunity to relieve both of your suffering.

From a naively ultimate point-of-view, every interaction with Another Being is to remind yourself of your own Inherent Freedom.

We might not consciously know or acknowledge this, but we are *all* influenced by these two point-of-views in our lives in some which way.

Think about your own self:

You do the best you can do to avoid and prevent suffering for yourself, while moving towards pleasure and what you think will make you happy.

You look for people and environments that will help you in some way whether:

Emotionally, financially, psychologically, and/or all 3.

We do our best to search for these kind of people and environments that we believe will bring us closer to our own Utopia of Well-Being.

We look for a base, a home from which we can prosper from.

The main issue is that too many people place importance on the external search of this apocryphal Well-Being, while completely disregarding our internal home that we forget is Free, Limitless, & Always Available.

We have forgotten how to access this internal space of Well-Being,

And now we are so distracted, stimulated, and influenced by externals that the internal is pushed by the wayside.

The thing we frequently overlook is this:

In the underpinnings of almost every human relationship, there is a secret hope that the other person will finally supply us with the peace, security, and happiness we are so desperately looking for.

We search and try, search and try, search and try, and nothing.

Essentially, we place the majority of our faith and efforts in finding peace, security, and happiness externally—which are all ultimately fleeting and momentary—while undermining what is Permanent and Free within.

Thus, why every relationship is doomed for some sort of disappointment from the outset.

Yes, this is all madness, I know.

Yet, it has plagued our ancestors before, and now pervades our era with ruthlessness.

We *all* carry this Freedom—this Sweet Unbounded Freedom—everywhere, yet squander and obscure it with our thoughts, expectations, and misdirected attention.

We forget that *we*, on a moment-to-moment basis, *choose* through the smallest of conscious and unconscious decisions, *what we place our Attention on.*

These small decisions end up forming one's mandala of Life (along with the Mysterious Forces out of one's "control").

Every thought, decision, action, and reaction fuse together in a beautiful moving mandala that is your self, your personality.

You live it and share it with Others wherever you go.

Make damn sure it's worth living and sharing.

"...no experience has been too unimportant, and the smallest event unfolds like a fate, and fate itself is like a wonderful, wide fabric in which every thread is guided by an infinitely tender hand and laid alongside another thread and is held and supported by a hundred others."

+ Rainer Maria Rilke, *Letters to a Young Poet*

ON CONTINUOUSLY DELUDING OURSELVES & OTHERS

September 21st, 30__

+ It just happens. We continuously delude ourselves and Others with our self-created worries, our learned misconceptions, and our unsubstantiated fears.

The majority of these stem from a constant process we all like to partake in which consists of: identifying *who you think you are* with the thoughts and stories that invariably run through your head.

(It's worth noting that most of our energy is usually and foolishly depleted by identifying with these thoughts.)

The Sages of History seem to agree that if we learn how to:

Wisely navigate through the nuanced veils of our thoughts and their convincing patterns, and observe who's the one actually thinking these thoughts, then one will discover that the thinker/ the ego/the believed-to-be-self is just a shadow, an enigma.

But, even upon just hearing these words does not equate full understanding.

One has to go on their own journey and find out for themselves.

The Truth is always present for the masses, but The Truth won't be understood by the masses.

It is only shown to, and later understood by, those who sincerely seek It.

"Belief is cheap.
Truth is dangerous, arduous, difficult; one has to pay for it.
One has to seek and search, and there is no guarantee that you will find it, there is no guarantee that there is any truth anywhere.
It may not exist at all."

+ Osho, *The Art of Living and Dying*

ON DISTILLED WISDOM FROM MASTER WY'S DISCOURSES, PT. 1

September 24th, 30__

+ A journal is a raw, visual map of one's internal landscape and its dynamics.

   The accuracy of the map depends on one's Unceasing Honesty and Humility.

+ Do not separate the Art you create with your current perception of Life.

   Your Life and your Art should move in Harmony to unlock the next Masterpiece.

+ Even in material wealth, surrounded by prosperity, one can still feel poor.

+ Avoid bad debt to all degrees, unless you wanna discover your labor tolerance and toil an indeterminate amount of time while wondering, each day, how long until all your debts are paid off. (Embrace and learn what good debt is, as the rich know how to masterfully do.)

+   What is one to do when one's usual distractions and entertainments inevitably lose their magnetic luster and meaningful appeal?

+   Create as if you'll die in 2 hours.

+   The words of a dead man are the sweetest.

+   Ask yourself: *How would I act if someone followed me with a video camera all day long?*

+   If I manage to arouse in you more questions than answers, I have fulfilled my Sacred Duty as a writer.

ON WRITING: (OBITER DICTUM)

September 26th, 30__

+ I write and I write and I write,

But yet, to what degree?

Why do I write?

Am I trying to get somewhere?

Do I write for the sake of writing itself?

Is it to give the appearance of a learned man to current and coming generations?

Is it because I'm trying to get to the bottom of my proclaimed personality and bust up its illusory beingness?

Is it because all these ideas and moods need to be released and recorded in some concrete form, taking on a life of their own, moving residence out of my mental landscape, and on to bigger and better things?

Is it because the only other people that will understand me live in books, who have also written because many Others in their own time period didn't fully understand them either?

* * *

At what point does one actually become a writer?

When one comes out with their first publication?

When one comes out with their second publication?

When one completes a whole notebook of writings?

When one becomes an English major?

When someone older than you, and of higher rank, claims you to be a writer?

Well, all of these are valid, but I'll weasel in my own answer now:

When you decide.

This applies to all Art and its respective Artists.

"Art never expresses anything but itself."

+ Oscar Wilde

ON "THE CLASSICS"

September 27th, 30__

+ There's this archaic, anxiety-laced fear that to be:

A learned man, a cultured person of the world,

One *must be* well-versed in "The Classics."

"The Classics," we're told, are the highest of heights regarding humanity's creative and mental prowess.

One *must be* well-versed in them to know what one is actually talking about.

I present myself here today calling BULLSHIT.

One more time:

B-U-L-L-S-H-I-T.

And while I do honor and revere "The Classics" (some of them) and their authors,

Too much faith and honor has been bestowed upon these works.

We treat them as if we are far separated from them and their "genius" artist(s), simultaneously convincing ourselves through this perception that we are incapable of creating similar works and beyond.

I whole-heartedly agree with Kierkegaard when he says:

> "When a human being possesses ethical strength,
> people like to elevate him into a genius, just to be rid of him;
> for his life constitutes a claim, a demand, on them."

It seems as if there's an inherent tendency within us,

That when we witness any Art that mystifies us, inculcates awe, or carries some sense of Other-Worldiness to it,

We want to label the creators of those works as geniuses,

As if to presume those geniuses are "out there,"

As if being a genius is "other,"

As if it's not inherent *within me*.

By doing this, one deludes themselves that being a genius is completely out of the cards for them, a gift only given to a few by chance.

With this perception, one is supposedly freed from having to create their own masterpiece.

Now, one thinks that they're off the hook from creating Art since they have separated themselves from the highest ideal they could be.

Beware of this perception—this façade of imprisonment—limiting one from reaching similar artistic heights.

We are all creators, now go create something wonderful.

ON DISTILLED WISDOM FROM MASTER WY'S DISCOURSES, PT. 2

September 30th, 30__

+ The lengths some men will go to search for sexual intercourse is a superpower in itself.

+ The lengths a writer will go to stall from writing is a superpower in itself.

+ Night seems to favor the artist.

+ Axioms, maxims, and aphorisms are the favored dialects of Intuition.

+ Temporary treatment for existential despair: cafés.

+ One writes mostly in 3 types of moods:

    1. When forced to and/or pretending to write something for the sake of pretending to write something.
    2. When one is inspired.
    3. When in the trenches of one's inescapable forlorn-melancholic-emptiness.

+ A toast can be thought of as collectively agreeing on the intention you're attributing to the liquid that you will all consume and become part of you.

+ I have never understood—and still do not understand—why people major in psychology when psychology's greatest lessons are found in family gatherings.

   The same goes for theater, playwriting, and philosophy majors.

> "If you think you're enlightened,
> go spend a week with your family."
>
> + Ram Dass

+ We misdirect much of our attention on thoughts and emotions of an illusory and constructed self,

   As opposed to directing that same attention *on being aware of our ability to be aware.*

   Most of us become so invested in the former narrative of an imaginary self, and neglect the latter view which is one of the only things that we can actually ever know:

   The knowing that some sort of knowing is happening right now.

"So before knowing what something is, if that is possible,
we must first come to the understanding that we do not know what
anything really is.

Therefore, the investigation into the nature of ourself
and the world of objects initially has more to do with the exposure
of deeply held ideas and beliefs about the way we think things are
than with acquiring any new knowledge.
It is the exposure of our false certainties…"

+ Rupert Spira

September 33rd, 30__

+ Our minds work like anthropological architects:

 Examining the past to construct a future.

+ Source speaks to us in every, every, every, every, every every, every, every single passing Moment.

 If one doesn't recognize this, then it is one's own fault.

+ Believe this, or believe this not,

 My writing this down is the highest activity I feel I can be performing right now.

 For some reason, *this is it*, this is the highest thing I can be doing in this current moment.

 Keep writing, keep creating.

 It all helps.

 It all helps.

September 36th, 30__

+ Each notebook, each page, each word, each letter, each movement, each breath is both an inquiry and its answer.

    Every word I utter, every act I perform, and every book I read are all attempts to understand my self, and when I say "my self" I really mean all selfs, and when I say "all selfs" I really mean No Self, and when I say "No Self" I really mean my self.

+ If Pure Intent and Pure Will radiate in balanced amounts within you, the people and the means to get you to where you need to go mysteriously effervesce from nowhere.

    Awareness, a keen sense of Awareness, is needed to recognize when this phenomenon occurs and how to act accordingly.

+ Life is a continuous lesson in how to live better.

+ Life is a continuous lesson in how to die better.

September 39th, 30__

+ Are we actually learning?

Where is the True Curriculum taught?

What does it look like?

How many edges does it contain?

Where?

When?

Why?

How?

Endless.

* * *

As Montaigne rightly warns:

Don't absorb information blindly.

Take what is useful for your self, for your growth and well-being, and leave the rest.

One will know when they have truly learned something when:

> "That which we rightly 'know' can be deployed without looking back at the model, without turning our eyes back towards the book."

+ When I die, please don't judge my notes nor my quotes,

　My best ideas were always thought of as I fell asleep.

CHAPTER
963 Hz

Remnants of Kizuku's Laundered Texts

(This notebook was rescued and transcribed from a small gray notebook which survived the watery wrath of a washing machine.)

A NOTEBOOK BEING WRITTEN IN

October 2nd, 30__

+ Can I write in this notebook just to write something down?

　Do I have permission?

　Oh, I do?

　Okay, sweet, then I'll humbly continue writing in this notebook because I now have permission to do so from an invisible authority I decided would allow me to continue writing in this notebook,

　Because this notebook is a notebook to be written in,

　And if it doesn't get written in for a while then it doesn't get written in for a while.

　What else is one to do when one's notebook is being written in?

　I'll get back to you on that because my notebook is currently being written in.

October 3rd, 30__

+ How does one give purpose to purpose?

Purpose.

Purpose.

How does one define one's purpose?

Well, we usually tend to define it according to one's current project(s), occupation(s), family, schooling, business, etc.,

But are those really enough to adequately define one's purpose?

Is that really the whole story?

Is purpose fluid?

Does it flux in its own seasons?

Does every human objectively share the same underlying Universal Purpose?

Or is it up to everyone's own subjective point-of-view to define purpose for their own self?

Both of these maybe?

Questions upon questions that need answers.

Who's going to answer them? "You?"

* * *

Can a scalding cup of hot apple cider give one purpose?

Now, to "whom" is this purpose being presupposed on?

Is this "whom" even that important?

Who are "they" to say what gives them purpose and what doesn't?

Now, zooming out, who is this observer observing this "whom?"

Does purpose and its defining now rest in the tender hands of this observer who's now observing this "whom" ascribing purpose to things?

How does one know if this observer observing isn't a different appearance of the same "whom?"

Who knows?

"Whom" doesn't, nor does the observer, two sides of the same coin.

So where does that leave us with purpose?

Nowhere, but *yet,* somewhere…

* * *

One could say purpose can be found in every passing moment, but what the fuck does that even mean?

Some will think it's a cute antidote for a couple moments.

For Others it'll serve as a momentary anesthetic.

So, let's not go with that already clichéd response.

How about:

Purpose can be found in whatever makes one's heart sing and dance with joyful serendipity.

Sure, cute attempt, but again, the similar frustrated response from before will probably present itself somewhere in the world, despite the fact that there's no escaping responses of that sort anyway.

So in essence—in an accelerated conclusion of sorts— it seems as if any answer can do because criticism will present itself anywhere.

No answer, no matter how outwardly perfect it looks, will ever be enough for everybody.

"For the meaning of life differs from man to man, from day to day and from hour to hour. What matters, therefore, is not the meaning of life in general but rather the specific meaning of a person's life at a given moment."

+ Viktor E. Frankl, *Man's Search For Meaning*

October 5th, 30__

Asked to Brother:

Kizuku: What is purpose?

Stephen: The reason…to…

To keep moving forward, to continue.

* * *

Unpremeditated text to a friend:

Kizuku: What is your definition of purpose, if you have one?

Caitlin: Purpose to me is giving meaning to a state of being.

Kizuku: And what motivates that definition of meaning to one's current state of being? What influences it?

Caitlin: The purity of emotion.

The awareness of the present, ever-changing.

The detachment or attachment to one's thoughts.

Many layers influence it.

This is all speculative however.

Attempts to give purpose to the word 'purpose' is pointless.

Purpose seems to be the surplus of judgments.

PARAPHRASED EXCERPT FROM DISCOURSE

October 7th, 30__

Kizuku: Please speak to me of death Master.

(silence)

Master Wy: The threat of death is one of our biggest wake-up calls in this Life.

Which memories will one remember best when they're older?

Why are some memories tinged with more vivacity than others?

Why does one choose to craft their Life through certain memories, ideas, and experiences rather than other memories, ideas, and experiences?

What are going to be the most probable thoughts racing across one's mental landscape at the moment of one's inescapable death?

- Did I live well?
- Did I accomplish everything I deemed necessary to accomplish?
- Has everything I've learned and studied been worth it for this moment of death? Was it worth learning while living?
- What will my family do without me? My kids?
- Did I fully share my every ounce of Love with them?
- Did I love myself enough?
- Did I love Others enough?

- Did I contribute anything positive to the world and to future generations?
- Will people's memories of me be consoling and nostalgic?
- Will I even be worth a memory?
- Will I be an inspiration for Others in some way?
- Did I blindly follow what I was told?
- Or did I live as truthfully as I could?

Deeply reflect on these questions.

Continue reminding yourself of them throughout your days.

How should you now live your Life after doing so?

What would you instantly change?

As the philosopher-king Marcus Aurelius wrote in his timeless book: *Meditations*:

"Human lives are brief and trivial.
Yesterday a blob of semen; tomorrow embalming fluid, ash."

THE APEX, THE APOGEE, THE CLIMAX

October 11th, 30__

+ Death will touch us all.

Some will know when, and Others will not.

What is certain is that *it comes when it comes*.

The Apogee, the Apex, the Climax of Life some regard it as.

I tip my hat to them and add one more thing to death's sullen description:

The Apogee, the Apex, the Climax of Life is at All Moments in Timelessness & Time.

Here, Then, There, Now, Here, Then, There, Now.

All. Right. Now.

We tend to only attribute the Climax of Life to death because it strips us of everything we thought we were.

We find out that all our masks were mere play toys limiting our Truest Essence from fully expressing Itself.

We find out that all our pretensions, quirks, frustrations, embarrassments, regrets, desires, vendettas, beliefs, and concepts were only masks—masks made out of wet sand loosely bound together by the glue of conformism,

All to be inexorably flushed down the Abyss of Understanding.

What is one left with?

Questions.

Questions that have been earnestly waiting eons to be asked:

"Why didn't I pay more attention while I was alive?"
"Why did I waste so much time?"
"Why was I so selfish?"
"Why wasn't I more honest?"
"Why wasn't I more sincere?"
"Why didn't I say 'Hi' more?"
"Why didn't I say 'Bye' more?"
"Why didn't I smile more?"
"Why didn't I laugh more?"
"Why didn't I cry more?"
"Why didn't I do more for myself?"
"Why didn't I do more for Others?"
"Why didn't I love my parents more?"
"Why didn't I love my siblings more?"
"Why didn't I love my friends more?"
"Why didn't I love my family more?"
"Why didn't I love Others more?"
"Why didn't I love myself more?"

For most, this is all an afterthought,

A moment too late,

A Life too late…

> "The tragedy of life is how little we end up living it."
>
> + Stephen Rozo

DAISY

+ I am in constant awe of the angel within the costume of my sweet Golden Labrador Retriever: *Daisy*.

   May she be remembered as one of the wisest dogs that has run its course on this terrestrial landscape.

   Patience, grace, wisdom, humility, humor, tenderness, and beauty radiates from her each and every ultra-fine golden hairs.

   Daisybabes.

   I fail to write about her more frequently because her poetry is recorded in her every step, in her every silence.

   Why would I bother to write about her when each of her movements extend into Infinity and back?

   Any written form to recreate them would be blasphemous at its core, kind of like what's happening right now...

2ND WEEK WITH MASTER WY: DISCOURSE NOTES

October 13th, 30__

+ Life: *The Recurring Cosmic Joke.*

    It eternally laughs at our dualistic paradoxes.

+ There's Inherent Humor everywhere we look.

    If it's not there, you're looking too hard.

+ All mental states are transient.

    One must travel to and experience the core of one's *essential beingness* to cut the roots of illness.

    If one doesn't find and sever these roots, they will be stuck on the branches trimming the ever-growing leaves forever.

+ Writing any story can be thought of as giving narrative form to one's internal/external happenings, through characters and situations.

> "A character is not a simulation of a living being. It is an imaginary being. An experimental self."
>
> + Milan Kundera, *The Art of the Novel*

+ Fruit should be shared when possible.

+ When you come home, greet your dog, and/or pet(s) first, not your fridge.

+ Anything kept in one's house should be kept for either of 2 reasons:

    1. It brings you and Others joy and meaning.
    2. It is of use for survival, utility, and/or hygiene.

    If it doesn't fall under these 2 categories, it's most likely extraneous.

+ Breathe with your entire body.

+ The only way to know space is to *be space*.

+ Anything that makes your heart melt is instantaneously virtuous.

+ When uncomfortable, seemingly awkward situations present themselves, don't hang your head and pretend not to see them. Look directly into the situation's eyes and find the paradox.

"Stick with the situation at hand, and ask,
'Why is this so unbearable?'
'Why can't I endure it?'
You'll be embarrassed to answer."

+ Marcus Aurelius

October 17th, 30__

+ We are all led—in varying degrees—by our senses:

Touch, taste, hearing, smell, sight, and feeling.

So, why do we jerk off and have sex?

Yes, I know, most likely to experience one of the highest feelings of pleasure one can experience in a human lifetime.

Yet, the case to make here is that many abuse this sexual freedom nowadays, and its intentions have denigrated into superficial forms of stimulating ourselves, naturally shifting the way we look at and treat women.

From this limited perspective, a woman is only a tool to satisfy a man and his own fleeting pleasures and emotions.

Yet, this isn't the whole story.

Sex is sacred, multidimensional in essence.

Women are to be respected and cared for.

They are our friends, our lovers, our sisters, our mothers.

Our sustenance.

We wouldn't be able to live without them.

Nor they without us.

- Fellas, here's a neat little exercise to try out:

  Imagine you don't have a penis anymore, would you still spend the amount of time you're spending on the person(s) you're currently talking to, chasing, and/or dating?

  Are you in love, or is your penis in love—in fervent search of its next pleasure?

  (Of course, this same exercise can be applied to women, making the necessary substitutions.)

October 19th, 30__

+ Mastery Wy sent me to work at a funeral home today.

 I learned 3 things:

 1) The fragility of Life

 2) The humor of Life.

 &

 3) Waiting.

 Waiting for what?

> LORD KRISHNA: "When they know that a day of Brahma
> stretches over a thousand eons,
> and his night ends in a thousand eons,
> men understand day and night."
>
> + *The Bhagavad-Gita*

ON WAITING

October 23rd, 30__

+ There is an art in waiting.

Who's waiting?

And what for?

Let's vivisect what waiting is and/or could be:

Scene: You're somewhere doing something, or nothing (one could argue that even doing nothing is still doing something). You're either expecting an expected and/or unexpected outcome to happen, at some point, whether it's waiting at your urologist's office, or waiting to go on stage to give a presentation on the epistemology of bat screeches.

Naturally, you wait.

So, why does waiting usually entail a negative connotation?

Why aren't we fully enjoying the moment right now and the proceeding ones after that one?

Why do we look to the future for this expected and/or unexpected outcome to happen as if this outcome will be the ultimate orgasm of our existence?

Ex. Think of yourself blowing up a bunch of balloons, and then trying to pop them all while complaining as to how they even got here, when it was you who blew them up in the first place.

This is what we do, repeatedly, throughout our days, with our thoughts, our desires, our expectations, our worries, and our fears.

We self-create and build all of this unnecessary tension in order to relieve it ourselves (or secretly hope that someone else will relieve it for us) at some point in the future.

Are we afraid to wait because most of us aren't comfortable with being alone with our thoughts for long periods of time?

I don't blame anyone.

It's terrifying being alone with one's continuous thought streams for long periods of time.

Especially since our contemporary society is structured upon cheap thrills and constant vacations of attention that distract us from feeling the Natural Isness of our Simple Beingness.

We're continuously telling ourselves deep down: "What's going to come up that I don't necessarily want to look at right now?"

> "I teach you the watcher. The only way to get out of misery patterns, whether ancient or new, is witnessing.
> I say it is the only way, because nobody has escaped from the mind without becoming a witness. Just witness, and suddenly you will start laughing at your own misery."

+ Osho

October 29th, 30__

+ Throughout your Life—specifically within certain time periods—you will feel certain inclinations to further study and/or go towards certain themes, subjects, people, places, things, and such:

E.g.: Movies, music, books, writers, history, countries, states, cities, celebrities, artists, scholars, friends, jobs, careers, hobbies, interests, etc.

On one level, you may understand the pull of whatever may be pulling you in its direction,

Or, you might not.

Despite the case, in my experience, you should follow the pull of whatever's magnetically enticing you.

The *why* is further explained sometime in the future.

"Only at the end (the end of love, of a life, of an era) does the past suddenly show itself as a whole and take on a brilliantly clear and finished shape."

+ Milan Kundera

October 31st, 30

+ Stop wasting your time using subpar, mediocre pens made by insincere assholes looking to profit.

 Go out and get yourself pens that you genuinely love and enjoy using.

 It is of paramount importance for a healthy and meaningful Life.

+ I want to personally meet the Director of this Whole Shenanigan.

 So many questions percolate to answers that will never, and/or not soon, be provided.

 Did God expect us to become this forgetful and ignorant?

 What's the failsafe measure He/She must've had to include?

WINNIE: "Yes, life I suppose, there is no other word."

+ Samuel Beckett, *Happy Days*

CHAPTER
174 Hz

Fabiano's Artist Journal

November 3rd, 30__

+ Every single word counts.

  Choose them carefully.

  Each word carves and lays the foundation for the next word that will duly carve and lay the foundation for the next word.

+ Observe which writers and artists you intimately resonate with.

  Why do you like their style? Their writing? Their Art?

  What are they trying to convey that you similarly want to convey?

> "A real writer (or artist or entrepreneur) has something to give. She has lived enough and suffered enough and thought deeply enough about her experience to be able to process it into something that is of value to others, even if only as entertainment."
>
> + Steven Pressfield

+ Ask yourself: *What do I want to express right now?*

  Now, go create it.

KƏ'THÄRSƏS

+ When experiencing any story, the observer of the story will inevitably be introduced to characters.

With this in play, the observer will naturally project their own values, behaviors, memories, and expectations onto each character, attempting to build them a unique personality-framework.

The observer naturally wants to see change.

The observer wants each character, who they just built a whole personality-framework around, to bust out of that framework and defy their expectations.

The observer attaches expectations and aspects of their own believed-to-be-self onto a character and then when that character grows and transcends those expectations and aspects for the better—or for the worse—

The observer explodes emotionally because they have vicariously identified an aspect of their believed-to-be-self with a character for that period of time.

This is how catharsis works.

"If I make you laugh at yourself, remember that my business as a classic writer of comedies is to 'chasten morals with ridicule'; and if I sometimes make you feel like a fool, remember that I have by the same action cured your folly."

+ George Bernard Shaw

- A story is the showing of a Being's transition between two or more worlds, and/or mental states,

  Moving from one world to another,

  From one mental state to another,

  Accompanied by some sort of transformation,

  While simultaneously reflecting an Intrinsic Remembrance of a familiar place.

- All characters are portrayals of mental states.

- A character should be a balance of complexity and simplicity:

  A walking paradox.

- Stay true to your Ideal Audience, meaning:

  The highest level of intelligence, wisdom, and understanding you think you know.

  Don't ever compromise your plot and/or story because you think a specific Other, and/or group of Others won't understand it.

  Any message will reveal itself to anyone it needs to be revealed to.

  All you are is the vehicle for its manifestation.

November 6th, 30__

+ What is not seen is always of interest.

+ You have to give the audience some sort of knowledge to create suspense.

   "There is no terror in the bang, only in the anticipation of it."

   + Alfred Hitchcock

+ Lose yourself in laughter.

   Lose the person holding on for dear life.

+ Listen.

+ Breathe.

+ If you know the Now, you simultaneously know the Future.

+ In an interview, director/writer Richard Linklater once said that he believes in Tarkovsky's belief in the idea that anything you fully invest yourself in while shooting a film or creating a work of art will inevitably be translated and felt, on an invisible level, by the spectator.

+ Film to watch before you die: *The Holy Mountain* by Alejandro Jodorowsky.

+ Book to read before you die: *Be As You Are* by Sri Ramana Maharshi, Edited by David Godman.

+ Patience: *the unchanging ability to accept things as they are.*

+ Don't follow me.

ON TEACHING

November 9th, 30__

+ Feelings of inadequacy constantly plague teachers of any sort through the guise of thought.

Thoughts ranging from:

- Am I teaching correctly?
- Is the student actually learning?
- Do I have enough credentials, or experience, to do this properly?
- Am I being too easy on the student?
- Am I being too hard on the student?
- Am I grading fairly? Correctly?
- Is my lesson sufficient for today? For the week?
- Am I enough?

"Am I enough?"

This seems to be the underlying thread interwoven through each of these questions.

"Am I complete enough as a human being to make my student feel as complete as they can?"

And, to be clear, when I use "make" in "make my student" I truly mean "inspire" because I cannot "make" a student do anything, nor can I "teach" a student anything.

I merely, as a teacher, facilitate their remembering and reassimilation of their Essential Being.

I give up on this game where I think I'm teaching people.

I'm teaching no one because there is no one to teach.

We All Know that We All Know.

Who am I to think that I know what's "right" and "wrong" to teach you?

I can somewhat guide.

I can somewhat point to something abstract.

But I cannot teach you anything new.

* * *

Most of the information presented to a student will most likely be discarded within the range of a couple seconds to a couple weeks (if one is so lucky).

So, with this, one naturally asks:

"What is the purpose in teaching if the information will be as quickly forgotten as the moments spent driving from one place to another?"

There is none. There is no purpose if we keep utilizing obsolete models of teaching.

Yet, *there is* purpose in teaching if we are able to connect the presented information with the student's current interests and current level of understanding.

"Socrates and then Archesilaus used to make their pupils speak first; they spoke afterwards....
It is good to make him trot in front of his tutor in order to judge his paces and to judge how far down the tutor needs to go to adapt himself to his ability.
If we get the proportion wrong we spoil everything; knowing how to find it and to remain well-balanced within it is one of the most arduous tasks there is.
It is the action of a powerful elevated mind to know how to come down to the level of the child and to guide his footsteps."

+ Michel de Montaigne

Integrate the information you need to present to the student, with information the student would want to hear and absorb into their Being.

If not, then you are only wasting time my dear friend.

Interest —> Processing —> Remembrance —> Application

There needs to exist a level of interest in both the student(s) and teacher, for the information to be properly processed, remembered, and applied.

If there isn't enough interest in a topic being taught then a student wouldn't even pass the processing phase, nor the remembrance and application phases either.

It can be safely said then, that *all of what teaching aims at is transforming a teaching to the application of the teaching, which is action.*

"If a person does not become what he understands, he does not really understand it."

+ Søren Kierkegaard

* * *

A few other purposes in teaching can include:

1) To clearly present information that one sincerely believes will add value and resonate with Another's Life and their native interests.

And:

2) To gently expose faulty thinking, and its associated conclusions, while being the conduit/mirror for the Other to find the answer themselves.

Any teacher—specifically those operating from a classroom—can easily lose sight of why they teach all these mounds of words and concepts to Others.

A teacher must continuously remind themselves of why they teach, and thus use this remembrance as a foundation for their day-to-day routines.

Don't even be afraid to question your foundations, for every foundation functions in an ethereal flux.

There is but only one Foundation that is truly Foundationless.

Follow That.

ON BITCOIN:
THE ART OF THIS NOT BEING
FINANCIAL ADVICE

November 12th, 30__

"It is no coincidence that the century of total war coincided with the century of central banking."

+ Ron Paul, *End the Fed*

+ Financial markets have the potential to show us how "enlightened" we really think we are.

  Observe your reaction(s) to each market dip and rise.

  How attached are you to your investments?

  What expectations underlie your attachments?

+ Blockchain technology is the digital form of Jung's collective unconscious.

+ God has elevated his game and now sends us Digital Sages.

+ Coders can now be considered as modern-day philosophers and economists.

- Highs,

    Lows,

    Just Watch Them All Go.

- HODLing (Holding On For Dear Life) is low-key a religion:

    A belief system anchored in faith that an asset will "save" one at a later date.

- We will tell the Bitcoin Tale to our kids, grandkids, and beyond.

- Bitcoin is the Tao in economic disguise.

    Bitcoin is the Tao in plain sight.

    Bitcoin is the Tao.

ASK YOURSELF

November 15th, 30__

+ What are you depending on?

 Why are you depending on it?

 What will it ultimately do for you?

ATTEMPTING TO FIND SOLITUDE IN MANICURED APHORISMS

November 17th, 30__

+ Aphorisms exist to succinctly pack a worthwhile understanding of Life into a catchy saying.

  The underlying premise seems to be to influence one's own future behavior, as well as Other's future behaviors as well.

  An aphorism is also a type of proof that you have understood something so convincing that you feel the need, and possess the required confidence, to share it with Others.

  And yet, the perfect aphorism is never enough.

  There is no all-pervasive aphorism that can sum up our moment-to-moment lives.

  Sure, finding a couple cuddly aphorisms written by some dude who died 102 years ago can temporarily help relieve one's suffering for a bit, I won't deny that.

  Knowing that someone else on Earth has come to a similar conclusion connects us with them in some intangible realm of understanding that allows Reality to intensify its Light through the gaps of our confidence.

  And now, we feel less alone in our personal convictions, and more confident in sharing and applying our newfound understandings with our current world.

  Yet, yet, despite this, they will never be a permanent solution.

Ultimately, we are alone to the end of our days.

Alone.

No matter how many people seem to surround us.

"The yardstick for a human being is: how long and to what degree he can bear to be alone, devoid of understanding with others."

+ Søren Kierkegaard

"What is necessary, after all, is only this: solitude, vast inner solitude. To walk inside yourself and meet no one for hours—that is what you must be able to attain."

+ Rainer Maria Rilke

- Many of us are currently afraid to create.

    We *all* receive intuitive impressions throughout our days, giving us the option to create those impressions into our physical existence.

    We *always* have the choice to create.

    Yet, many limit themselves through fearful conditioning and self-defeating thoughts that obstruct their potential creations from ever being created into our physical existence and subsequently shared with Others.

    We must remind ourselves that there is a niche for everything.

    And that everything, *everything*, is an opportunity to create.

November 18th, 30__

+ All that language really is: are sounds infused with meaning.

WORDS

They Live!

They Die.

WORDS

+ Surrounded by questions, the mind constructs its array of confusion in appealing packets of curiosity, masking its main agenda:

To increase separation.

* * *

My Muse, My Sweet Beautiful Muse,
Where Might You Reside?

I wait, and wait, and wait
For your Subtle Presence to illuminate this frame—
To move in harmony with
The Music of The Spheres.

I know it exists, I know it does,
Because I have heard The Music
And Danced with The Spheres.

* * *

CHAPTER
285 Hz

The Muse's Musings

(This student has requested to remain anonymous.)

December 3rd, 30__

+ It is not only until you experience this madness of suffering over and over and over and over and over again that one realizes, ever so gradually, that *it* is in fact: *madness.*

What is this *it*, this suffering?

Why do we suffer?

Who is the one suffering?

Who keeps trying to grasp each and every thought that gets picked up by our body's antennas?

Who keeps trying to grasp the varying projections of Love, Security, Peace, and Purpose through things in our world?

Who continues to grasp as if some external thing "out there" will finally reconcile this unnerving feeling of lack and suffering continuously being peddled by one's habitual thought and nervous system patterns?

Why do I keep choosing to suffer moment after moment?

Is it even a choice?

"To realize that our knowledge is ignorance,
This is a noble insight.
To regard our ignorance as knowledge,
This is mental sickness.

Only when we are sick of our sickness
Shall we cease to be sick.
The Sage is not sick, being sick of sickness;
This is the secret of health."

+ Lao Tzu, *Tao Teh Ching*

December 6th, 30__

+ Whenever you witness an Other in The Midst Of It All: confusion, pain, fear, and suffering of all natures.

Remind yourself of your last visit into The Midst Of It All.

What did you want at that moment?

* * *

Whenever in the midst of suffering, just create.

Create Art.

Create Anything.

Your soul sings in its Highest Ecstasy whenever creating.

It yearns for It Moment after Moment.

Create Art.

Create Anything.

Liberate your Self of your imaginary self.

Liberate Others of their imaginary self.

Create Art.

Create Anything.

We're All in this Together.

December 9th, 30__

\+ I am a Word Painter.

I paint the words of my Perpetual Freedom.

December 12th, 30__

+ There always seems to be one more thing to do until all is finally in its place…

   That is, until the next thing appears.

December 15th, 30__
11:11 am

+ Beautiful start to the day.

    The birds are chirping.

    The wind is swaying.

    The pen is dancing.

    This Whole Thing continues.

+ We are all given Life to create, experiment, and celebrate.

    That's it.

    Oh, and to Love as well.

December 16th, 30__

- + We are continuously making Love with the Universe everywhere we go.

- + The only thing we can ever truly offer another being is our kiss of attention.

"The morning wind forever blows,
the poem of creation is uninterrupted;
but few are the ears that hear it."

+ Henry David Thoreau

THE WILL TO WRITE. THAT'S IT.

December 17th , 30__

Contractions contracting the constricting tubules of blood and vinegar being wiped off the counter for heaven's sake.

"Clean up after the cook."
The wisest advice an ornithologist once confided in me.

Deceiving the deceiver with tricks up the sleeve,
Of places Unknown & Near.

Hear-ho! Hear-ho! Hear-ho!

The Sound of Freedom rings through one's cells.

Hear-ho! Hear-ho! Hear-ho!

What of you old chap?
The wintry sunrise invites no one to its forest.
Eat up! There's plenty for everyone.

Let what is, is.
For nothing is nothing until it's something.
And something isn't nothing until it's something.

For what do sun-dried tomatoes have to do with the occasion?

Everything.

Although, it doesn't in fact exist.

"How can it not exist if it was just said?"

Forlorn is the answer to the riddle.
(Good thing The Riddler arose today.)

"Malfeasance! On the part of the King," the plebeian plead to the plentiful patrons.

He continued, "The Kingdom has been cost! Ring thee alarms!"

Ring! Ring! Ring! Ring!

Ring only exists in a story, with its twists and turns.

Whose choice is it anyway?

The mallard's? or The goose's?

EVERYTHING DOESN'T NEED A TITLE

December 18th, 30__

AMNESIA

December 19th, 30__

We are living,

But it seems as if we've forgotten.

We are also dying,

Dying in forgetfulness.

I HAVE ALL THE ANSWERS

December 20th, 30__

Please, listen to me, please.
I have *all* the answers, please.
I know it all., please.
I know it all, please.
Please, listen to me, please.

I have all the answers to Absolutely Nothing.

December 21st, 30__

+ Is a thing just a thing because it's a thing?

Aristotle believed that every single thing in this world has a *telos*:

An Inherent Goal and Meaning everything in Existence seems to uniquely contain, and continuously move towards.

Anything ranging from ourselves, to a platypus, to a ukulele, apparently has a *telos*.

I agree.

"Exactly the same is happening in this chair and the same is happening underneath you in the floor.
It is not a marble floor, that is only an appearance, but the energy particles are moving so fast that their very movement, their fastness, creates the illusion of substance.
Substance exists not, only pure energy exists."

+ Osho

December 22nd, 30__

+ A plethora of divergently homogenous replicas of The Big Guy Upstairs, G_D, YAHWEH, Our One & Only Father, The Lord, Jesus Christ, Buddha, Allah, Brahma, Shiva, Vishnu, The Tao, The Universe, Energy, Source, Atoms, The Present Moment, The Ancient One, The Now, The Void, The Sound Of One Hand Clapping, Nothingness, & Oneness abound with Abundance.

    Everywhere I go, everywhere I look, a different person with a different face, with a different hairstyle, with a different attire, with a different demeanor, and a different personality consumes my attention for a few split seconds until the same process repeats for the next person, and the next, and the next...

    A Paradox within a Paradox paradoxing.

+ Epistemology is an interesting branch of philosophy.

    How do we know that we *actually* know something? Or anything for that matter?

    Which assumptions do we take to be self-evident?

    Which assumptions do we take to be non-negotiable?

    Have we ever *truly* and *honestly* questioned our own beliefs and opinions of the world around us?

December 23rd, 30__

- Sincerity

    Honesty

    &

    Attention

    Are The Keys To Freedom

- Pursue The Truth until it hurts no more.

- Another Day, Another Opportunity to Live Truth.

    Another Day, Another Opportunity to Reveal A Facet of Ignorance I've Chosen To Believe Over & Over Again.

- Ask yourself:

    If I had the ability to meet God, what would I say?

    What would I ask for?

December 24th, 30__

+ The process of human thought can be viewed as belonging to either of two categories:

You are either:

1) Creating a brand new piece of dialogue (thought pattern) with an attached story.

And/or:

2) Continuing the story of a previously created dialogue (thought pattern).

Watch thoughts.

And find their Original Source.

December 25th, 30__

- Nobody knows anything other than the Knowing that we are currently having this Experience on Earth.

    Therefore, everything we do is constant experimentation,

    Even our habits.

    They're just longer-term experiments.

- Art is the organic outgrowth of expressing one's Understanding.

- Art is relieving one's self, and Others, out of their mental prisons and introducing them back to Reality.

- Art is the Divine expressed in its Endless Emanations.

- An Artist is he or she who is porous enough to dip into the Collective Unconscious we all share and creates something with the information they come back with.

    The Brave are those who come back from their journeys and share their creations with us all.

"Once the artist has had a mystical experience, the task is to integrate the visions and energy of this state into the physical act of making art. The artist brings the infinite into finite form, compressing absolute reality into the relative phenomenal field of appearances. The deeper the individual artists penetrate into their own infinitude, the more able they are to transmit that state. The artist relies on visionary revelations that point to the spiritual ideal beyond mundane perception. By externalizing these revealed symbols in art objects, the artist provides a crystallized passage back to the mystic visionary state."

+ Alex Grey, *The Mission of Art*

+ There comes a crucial point in an Artist's experience in which his or her natural inclination to study the Greats and Other's work doesn't interest, nor satisfy him/her as it did before.

    This inevitably leads the Artist to create their own masterpieces that will fulfill themselves, and Others inadvertently.

+ Our Lives: our physiology, psychology, phenomenology, and sociology all work in cycles.

    Round and round and round the Same Wheel.

+ We are only ever communicating with ourselves.

+ Everything one creates is a device to express and redirect one's Attention back Home: the effortless resting as Spaciousness in the *entire* body.

+ We, *generally*, do not seek information.

    We seek permission.

    A leader is just someone who continuously gives themselves permission to experiment, fail, do, and *be* more than a "follower."

    And the leader—in seeing Others get caught in this trap of limiting themselves—guides them out of their delusion.

December 31st, 30__

Student: Master, I've had this suspicion for a long time that there was something beyond our minds and the corresponding thoughts that seemingly create our identity, but I could never quite pinpoint it. I've attempted to convey this to Others, yet few seem to grasp what I'm saying. Why is this so?

(silence)

Mastery Wy: Would you like to go to the mall with me later?

Student: Master, you know I strongly dislike going to the mall.

Master Wy: But, I love going to the mall.

Student: But what does that have to do with—oh…

Master Wy: Everyone is attracted to what they are attracted to.

One may be able to explain why, and one may not.

(silence)

This may be the hardest concept to digest from our time together, yet I feel the need to say it in this moment.

I have never intimated this to anybody, and I am not a proponent of placing types of people into trivial categories and/or compartments, but for the purpose and nature of your question I will make an exception.

None of these theoretical formulations should imply that one is superior to another, nor that these exemplify actual types of people.

They are all equally valuable and have their place and purpose.

So, here are 3 extremely general and extremely trivial categories, where, in my experience on this Earth, I have observed characteristics of people generally fit into:

The 1st Group:

Those who rarely question where they come from, where they're going to, and what their purpose on Earth is.

This group tends to follow their lives in blind obedience to their minds and bodies, repeating pattern after pattern after pattern of their own suffering, slaves to the whims of their nervous system.

They continuously feel as if the world is against them.

They continuously ask why there is so much evil present in the world.

They continuously complain and argue as much as they feel is necessary.

They live their day-to-day lives in constant conflict, which they unconsciously feel, on some level, gives them a sort of purpose.

These people spend the majority of their mental energy ruminating on memories of the past and worrying about the future.

Ultimately, these are Thoreau's people who "live lives of quiet desperation," who regret their whole Life when on their deathbed.

This is the group I have the most compassion for.

The 2nd Group:

A smaller minority of people with slight curiosities to search for The Truth, but then having these curiosities squashed by societal pressures, psychological conditionings, family, or whichever the case may be.

These are the people who are presented, at some point in their lives, the opportunity to take the blue pill or the red pill. They are given the choice to jump down the rabbit hole of Searching For Truth, or not.

These people inherently know there is something beyond their minds, but are too afraid to jump into The Unknown and either quit from the start of their journey, halfway, or don't begin The Search at all.

Their habitual mental tendencies tend to outweigh the desire to be free from their mind's imprisonment.

A few from this group, unlike the majority of the 1st group, actually have a choice to either follow The Search For Truth or not.

The 3rd Group:

The minorities of the minority: *The Seekers of Truth*.

These are *those* who have an inkling that there are "more things in heaven and earth than are dreamt of in one's own philosophy."

These are *those* who live a portion of their lives in ignorance, and then ignited with some type of catalyst that reminds them of something beyond who they think they are.

These are *those* who read book after book searching for the person who has figured it all out, the concept that will explain everything to us with clarity.

These are *those* who travel the globe extensively, realizing that Truth is nowhere to be found externally without integrating and reconciling the internal beforehand.

These are *those* who understand that: "One whose mouth has actually tasted molasses, does not need others to explain its taste."

These are *those* who search for Truth with ceaselessness and vigor, not knowing that their very seeking creates the whole problem in the first place.

These are *those* who understand Ramana Maharshi when he says: "There is no reaching the Self. If Self were to be reached, it would mean that the Self is not here and now and that it is yet to be obtained. What is got afresh will also be lost. So it will be impermanent. What is not permanent is not worth striving for."

And finally, these are *those* who ultimately realize that:

The Search for Enlightenment is like being a person on a boat in the sea, searching for the person, the boat, and the sea.

(silence)

Student: (*strikes Master Wy in the face*)

(silence)

Master Wy: (*smiles*) Thank you Master.

"'Have you guessed the riddle yet?'
the Hatter said, turning to Alice again.
'No, I give it up,' Alice replied: 'what's the answer?'
'I haven't the slightest idea,' said the Hatter.
'Nor I,' said the March Hare."

+ Lewis Carroll, *Alice's Adventures in Wonderland*

DEDICATED TO:

My Mother, for everything

My Brothers, Stephen & Jonathan, for everything

My Father, for everything

My Daisybabes, for everything

My Family, for everything

Caitlin DeBartolo, Junior Cordeiro, Matthew McCarthy, & Cassie Urban, for friendship, laughter, and support

Ari Selinger, for friendship and inspiration

Lena Nagorna, for friendship and your love of dedication pages (This page wouldn't exist if it wasn't for your wise suggestion)

The Centerless Center

The Formless Space Within Borders & Beyond Them

My Invisible, Visible Teacher(s)

AUTHOR'S MEMORANDUM:

Thank you for being here.

And, most importantly, thank you for your attention.

For those who resonated with anything in this book, and are interested in finding freedom in the mind, the body, and who are searching for a clearer way to live, please do not hesitate in reaching out.

With Love & Attention,

Sebastian James Rozo

FOR GENEROUS DONATIONS:

Bitcoin:

Public Key: 3NFYa1GUiBUKR8xUMAwfSG7Qc7LuVKc7pt

Litecoin:

Public Key: MM8wW18YDusW99MVspcoxCPADpk3ohaeti

CONTACT:

Instagram: @thebelievedtobeself

Website: www.thebelievedtobeself.com

Email: thebelievedtobeself@gmail.com

Bibliography

Thoreau, Henry David. *Walden, or, Life in the Woods*. Dover Publications, 1995.

Woolf, Virginia. *A Room of One's Own*. Harcourt Brace Jovanovich, 1957.

CHAPTER 396 Hz

Dogen, and Shohaku Okumura. *Dogen's Genjo Koan: Three Commentaries*. Counterpoint, 2011.

Gide, Andre. *The Counterfeiters*. Vintage Books, 1973.

Khayyam, Omar, and Edward FitzGerald. *Rubaiyat*. Crowell, 1964.

Michel de Montaigne and M. A. Screech. "To Philosophize Is to Learn How to Die." *The Complete Essays*, Penguin Books, 1993.

Montaigne, Michel de, and M. A. Screech. *The Complete Essays*. Penguin Books, 1993.

Spira, Rupert. *The Transparency of Things: Contemplating the Nature of Experience*. Sahaja, 2016.

Wilde, Oscar. "The Soul of Man Under Socialism." *The Soul of Man under Socialism and Selected Critical Prose*. Edited by Linda Dowling, Penguin Books, 2001.

CHAPTER 417 Hz

Caputi, Anthony. *Eight Modern Plays: The Wild Duck, Three Sisters, Candida, the Ghost Sonata, Six Characters in Search of an Author, Long Day's Journey into Night, Mother Courage and Her Children, Happy Days: Backgrounds and Criticism*. W.W. Norton, 1991.

Cooper, David A. *The Heart of Stillness: the Elements of Spiritual Practice*. Bell Tower, 1992.

Heidegger, Martin, et al. *Being and Time*. HarperPerennial/Modern Thought, 2008.

Kierkegaard, Søren. *The Diary of Søren Kierkegaard*. Edited by Peter P. Rohde, Citadel Press, 2000.

Laozi, and Brian Browne Walker. *Hua Hu Ching: The Unknown Teachings of Lao Tzu*. HarperOne, 2009.

Montaigne, Michel de, and M. A. Screech. *The Complete Essays*. Penguin Books, 1993.

Thoreau, Henry David. *Walden, or, Life in the Woods*. Dover Publications, 1995.

Watson, Burton, translator. *The Complete Works of Zhuangzi*. Columbia University Press, 2013.

Wilde, Oscar. "The Soul of Man Under Socialism." *The Soul of Man under Socialism and Selected Critical Prose*. Edited by Linda Dowling, Penguin Books, 2001.

Wittgenstein, Ludwig, and Bertrand Russell. *Tractatus Logico-Philosophicus*. Routledge, 2001.

CHAPTER 528 Hz

Henry David Thoreau. "Where I Lived, and What I Lived For." *Walden, or, Life in the Woods*, Dover Publications, 1995.

Miller, Barbara Stoler. *The Bhagavad-Gita: Krishna's Counsel in Time of War*. Bantam Books, 2004.

CHAPTER 639 Hz

Calvino, Italo. *Six Memos for the Next Millennium*. Harvard University Press, 1988.

Durant, Will. *The Story of Philosophy: The Lives and Opinions of the Great Philosophers of the Western World*. Simon and Schuster, 2009.

Gibran, Kahlil. *The Prophet*. Alfred A. Knopf, 1923.

Nietzsche, Friedrich. *Basic Writings of Nietzsche*. Translated by Walter Kaufmann, Modern Library, 2009.

Sartre, Jean-Paul. *Existentialism Is a Humanism*. Yale University Press, 2007.

CHAPTER 741 Hz

Brahmachari, Shuddhanandaa. *The Incredible Life of a Himalayan Yogi*. Edited by Ann Shannon, Lokenath Divine Life Mission, 2016.

Calvino, Italo. *Six Memos for the Next Millennium*. Harvard University Press, 1988.

Kabat-Zinn, Jon. *Wherever You Go, There You Are: Mindfulness Meditation in Everyday Life*. Hachette Books, 2010.

Kundera, Milan. *The Art of the Novel*. Translated by Linda Asher, Harper Perennial, 2006.

Lucretius, *De Rerum Natura*, iii. 1093.

Russell, Bertrand. *A History of Western Philosophy*. Simon and Schuster/Touchstone, 1967.

CHAPTER 852 Hz

Caputi, Anthony. *Eight Modern Plays: The Wild Duck, Three Sisters, Candida, the Ghost Sonata, Six Characters in Search of an Author, Long Day's Journey into Night, Mother Courage and Her Children, Happy Days: Backgrounds and Criticism.* W.W. Norton, 1991.

Dass, Ram. "Ram Dass Quotes." *RamDass.org*, 2 Apr. 2015, www.ramdass.org/ram-dass-quotes/.

Kierkegaard, Søren. *The Diary of Søren Kierkegaard.* Edited by Peter P. Rohde, Citadel Press, 2000, p. 123.

Miller, Barbara Stoler. *The Bhagavad-Gita: Krishna's Counsel in Time of War.* Bantam Books, 2004.

Montaigne, Michel de, and M. A. Screech. *The Complete Essays.* Penguin Books, 1993, p. 45.

Osho. "Caveat: The Problem of Belief." *The Art of Living and Dying,* Watkins Publishing, 2013.

Rilke, Rainer Maria. *Letters to a Young Poet.* Translated by Mary D. Herter Norton, W. W. Norton & Company, 1993.

Rumi, Jalal al-Din. "Quietness." *The Essential Rumi.* Translated by Coleman Barks, HarperOne, 2004.

Shakespeare, William, and Paul Werstine. *As You Like It.* Edited by Barbara A. Mowat, Simon & Schuster, 2004.

Spira, Rupert. *The Transparency of Things: Contemplating the Nature of Experience.* Sahaja, 2016.

Wilde, Oscar. "De Profundis." *The Soul of Man & Prison Writings.* Edited by Isobel Murray, Oxford University Press, 1999.

Wilde, Oscar. "The Decay of Lying." *The Soul of Man under Socialism and Selected Critical Prose*. Edited by Linda Dowling, Penguin Books, 2001.

CHAPTER 963 Hz

Aurelius, Marcus. *Meditations: A New Translation*. Translated by Gregory Hays, Modern Library, 2003.

Caputi, Anthony. *Eight Modern Plays: The Wild Duck, Three Sisters, Candida, the Ghost Sonata, Six Characters in Search of an Author, Long Day's Journey into Night, Mother Courage and Her Children, Happy Days: Backgrounds and Criticism*. W.W. Norton, 1991.

Frankl, Viktor E. *Man's Search for Meaning*. Beacon Press, 2006, p. 108.

Kundera, Milan. *The Art of the Novel*. Translated by Linda Asher, Harper Perennial, 2006.

Miller, Barbara Stoler. *The Bhagavad-Gita: Krishna's Counsel in Time of War*. Bantam Books, 2004.

Osho. T*he Art of Living and Dying*, Watkins Publishing, 2013, p. 78.

CHAPTER 174 Hz

Attributed to Hitchcock in *Halliwell's Filmgoer's Companion* (1984).

Barnet, Sylvani: Eds. Berman Morton; Burton William. *Type of Drama, Plays and Essays*. Boston: Little Brown and Boston, 1972.

Kierkegaard, Søren. *The Diary of Søren Kierkegaard*. Edited by Peter P. Rohde, Citadel Press, 2000, p. 121.

Kierkegaard, Søren. *The Diary of Søren Kierkegaard*. Edited by Peter P. Rohde, Citadel Press, 2000, p. 126.

Montaigne, Michel de, and M. A. Screech. *The Complete Essays*. Penguin Books, 1993, p. 43.

Pressfield, Steven. *Nobody Wants to Read Your Sh*t: Why That Is and What You Can Do About It*. Black Irish Entertainment LLC, 2016, p. 50 - 51.

Rilke, Rainer Maria. *Letters to a Young Poet*. Translated by Mary D. Herter Norton, W. W. Norton & Company, 1993.

Ron Paul. "Central Banks and War." *End the Fed*, Grand Central Publishing, 2010, p. 63.

CHAPTER 285 Hz

Carroll, Lewis. *Alice's Adventures in Wonderland*. Random House UK, 2016.

Coleman, Graham. *The Tibetan Book of the Dead - First Complete Translation*. Edited by Thupten Jinpa. Translated by Gyurme Dorje, Penguin Classics, 2007.

Grey, Alex. *The Mission of Art*. Shambhala, 2001, p. 117.

Maharshi, Ramana, and David Godman. *Be As You Are: The Teachings of Sri Ramana Maharshi*. Arkana (Penguin Books), 1985.

Osho. "Responses to Questions." *The Art of Living and Dying*, Watkins Publishing, 2013, p. 64.

Thoreau, Henry David. *Walden, or, Life in the Woods*. Dover Publications, 1995.

Tzu, Lao. *Tao Teh Ching*. Translated by John C. H. Wu, Shambhala Publications Inc, 2006.

Copyright © 2018 Sebastian Rozo

The Awakened Moment

All rights reserved.

ISBN - 13: 978-0-692-15047-4

ISBN - 10: 0-692-15047-1

To Know Is To Know That You Don't Know

by

Sebastian James Rozo

www.ingramcontent.com/pod-product-compliance
Lightning Source LLC
Chambersburg PA
CBHW022112040426
42450CB00006B/663